Zoë
Cambridge. Feb. 1995

Masterplan

Masterplan

*How God makes sense
of the world*

Roy Clements

Inter-Varsity Press

INTER-VARSITY PRESS
38 De Montfort Street, Leicester LE1 7GP, England

First published 1994

British Library Cataloguing in Publication Data

A catalogue record for this book is available from the British Library.

ISBN 0-85110-876-8

Set in 10 on 12½ point Linotron Palatino
Typeset in Great Britain by Parker Typesetting Service, Leicester
Printed in Great Britain by Cox & Wyman Ltd, Reading

Inter-Varsity Press is the book-publishing division of the Universities and Colleges Christian Fellowship (formerly the Inter-Varsity Fellowship), a student movement linking Christian Unions in universities and colleges throughout the United Kingdom and the Republic of Ireland, and a member movement of the International Fellowship of Evangelical Students. For information about local and national activities write to UCCF, 38 De Montfort Street, Leicester LE1 7GP.

Contents

Part four: New creation

Publisher's foreword

Overviews of life, the universe, and everything have become very popular. They range from Stephen Hawking's *A Brief History of Time*, in which he tried to touch the 'mind of God', to Douglas Adams' comic series, *The Hitch-Hiker's Guide to the Galaxy*, in which the meaning of the universe turned out to be the number forty-two.

Such brief overviews can easily be a grotesque over-simplification. Surely things are much more complex than this. Yet they do show that it is possible to look at life, the world and history from one specific angle and express it briefly, clearly and imaginatively.

This is what Dr Roy Clements did when he presented the talks that are the basis of this book at a student conference, *Manchester 90*. He spotlighted the basic elements in God's plan for creation, the fall of humanity at the beginning of history, and God's redemption and new creation. These elements make up the biblical story which ranges over all history, including the future.

A firm grasp of this outline will be an enormous help to Christians who are trying to fit a multitude of ideas and biblical doctrines together, to enquiring minds needing to view the wood as well as the trees, and to doubters who might now see that there is some logic and plausibility to this view of the cosmos after all.

We are all looking for an explanation that does justice to our human experience of the world. Here is a reasonable, exciting and understandable outline by a theological scientist with more than a touch of the poetic. Enjoy it.

Part one

Creation

1

Monkeys and bishops

The controversy had been brewing in academic circles for well over a century, but it was in June 1860 that the storm really broke as far as the general public were concerned. That was when Bishop Wilberforce of Oxford had a public debate with Professor T. H. Huxley of Imperial College in London. The Bishop concluded his address by sarcastically asking the Professor whether he claimed descent from a monkey on his mother's or his father's side. Huxley replied that he would not much mind a monkey for an ancestor but he would be ashamed to be affiliated to certain bishops he could name. So the battle was joined. It hit the headlines. Was the world, this marvellous world, and the human race in particular, the result of natural evolution or was it the result of a divine creation?

Over the years the battle has been confused by both sides rather exaggerating their case. Scientists have their limitations. Until the arrival of Dr Who's time machine there is no way anyone can comment on the origin of man without relying very heavily on speculation and unprovable assumptions. Scientists have often overestimated the objectivity of their opinions in this field, failing to recognize how profoundly their own philosophical assumptions colour their theories.

What's more, the evidence for natural evolution is not as overwhelmingly compelling as biological textbooks sometimes imply. Cladistics, a new way of classifying living things, has in recent years called into question much conventional evolutionary history. The fossil evidence is by no means as complete or as unambiguous as is sometimes implied. And perhaps most interesting of all, mathematical calculations on the probability of the spontaneous generation of life from inorganic materials in a primeval soup have led many scientists to doubt the statistical plausibility of neo-Darwinian evolution. The odds against it happening that way seem just too enormous to be believable.

Some Christians, of course, eagerly seize on these weaknesses and write books on seven-day creation and a young earth. But Christians have their limitations too. The Bible is a book that cannot be understood without the employment of fallible human reason, and that means that it is perfectly possible to interpret the Bible wrongly. There have been some notable examples throughout church history of Christians doing just that. Christians have often exaggerated the clarity of the Bible on this issue of origins, failing to accept the admissibility of more than one valid understanding of the early chapters of Genesis.

What kind of literature?

Just take Genesis 1, for instance. To what literary

type does it belong? Is it poetry, like David's psalms? There is a parallelism in the structure of Genesis 1, the first three days speaking of the emergence of light and sea and land, and the last three days speaking of light-bearers in the heavens, marine life in the oceans and then animal life upon the land.

Or could it be a vision, corresponding to John's vision in the book of Revelation at the other end of the Bible? Genesis 2 does mention the tree of life, and that's a symbol that recurs in Revelation 22.

Or could it be a prophetic message, a word from God about the past, as Jeremiah and Isaiah were favoured with words from God about the future? The authorship of Genesis, after all, is ascribed to the greatest prophet of them all, Moses.

Or could it be a theological tract, deliberately composed to counter the mythological accounts of origins which threatened the Hebrew faith in the ancient world, by stressing the supremacy and priority of Jehovah over all the cosmic forces of pagan astrology and religion?

It is all very well to say we take the Bible literally, but that does not mean that we take no account of the different kinds of literature that the Bible contains. Poetry often uses metaphor. Visions often use symbol. Prophecy is often given in a time-collapsed form, and theology is much more interested in the doctrine of God than in the facts of science. Interestingly, the one category into which it is very difficult to put Genesis 1 is history, because biblical history, just like any other history, always depends upon human eye-witness testimony. The books of Samuel or the books of Kings draw on human sources of memory and tradition, and by definition such memory is out of the question where Genesis 1 is concerned.

History cannot really begin in the proper sense of that word until Genesis 2, with the arrival of Adam and Eve. Whether you regard them as real people or prefer to see them as symbolic figures, it is obvious that they represent what anthropologists would identify as neolithic culture. They are not hunters, they are gardeners. They do not roam like nomads, they live in one place and have a settled existence. So we have to conclude that the Bible shows absolutely no interest in creatures that existed before the dawn of neolithic culture, fifteen or twenty thousand years BC. As far as Genesis is concerned that's when the history of *homo sapiens* began. On the vexed question of dinosaurs and Neanderthal apes, Genesis draws a veil of silence. So in this book we shall do the same!

They've missed the point

The fact is that both scientists and Bible students have on occasion lacked the intellectual humility necessary to both their disciplines. Controversy is always rendered more acrimonious when those who are unable to strengthen their arguments resort simply to raising their voices, and over the years Genesis 1 and 2 have been the focus of a great many shouting matches of that kind. And ironically, it has often been to no great purpose. The debate has been misdirected; it has missed the point. The technical question of how and when the human race originated is a trivial one, in comparison to the much more fundamental and important issue of the nature and destiny of the human race. Perhaps an illustration will help.

Suppose you received a mysterious letter. It is written in an unknown hand and in a foreign language. It bears an exotic stamp. You could give it to a scientist, and he would no doubt tell you a lot about the letter. He could do various tests on the ink and try to establish how long ago the letter had been written. He could examine the stamp and try to identify the country of origin. He might even look at the handwriting and present you with a personality profile of the author. But then you say to him, 'Well, that's all very interesting, but what does the letter say?' The scientist replies, 'Don't ask me! Take that question to the linguistics department. As far as I'm concerned it's just a random collection of meaningless marks.'

In the same way, scientists may offer their learned judgments about when and where the human race began, but the most vital question for you and me is not the *origin* of mankind but the *meaning* of mankind. Who am I? Why am I here? Where am I going? There is no way that experiments on fossilized bones can answer that kind of question. And when scientists pass their opinions on such matters they are going beyond science and into the realm of philosophy and metaphysics and religion, where they are no more qualified than anyone else. Yet, of course, there is no way we can avoid asking such questions. For we are human beings. For us these are not abstract theoretical issues but crucial existential ones. If we don't understand the meaning of mankind, we do not understand ourselves, and we demand such an understanding.

For whatever the truth about evolution may be, man is different from the animals, at least in this regard. He is not content simply to survive. He demands a sense of purpose. He insists that life must have a meaning. And science cannot tell him what that meaning is. It cannot read the letter. But Genesis can. Genesis can translate the mysterious epistle of our human existence and tell us what it says. When you do not understand a novel, do not ask the critics, ask the author. When you do not understand yourself, do not ask the scientist – he is as confused as you are – ask your Creator. What we have in Genesis is a word from God to explain to us just who we are. If we could have worked it out on our own he would not have bothered to tell us, but he has taken pity on our ignorance and delivered us from it through revelation:

> 'Let us make man in our image, in our likeness, and let them rule over the fish of the sea and the birds of the air, over the livestock, over all the earth, and over all the creatures that move along the ground.' So God created man in his own image, in the image of God he created him; male and female he created them.
>
> (Gn. 1:26–27)

2

Machines or animals?

Genesis claims that the human race is God-like, that it is made in the image of God. This is true of no other part of God's creation.

Over the past century science has explored two models for the categorization of mankind. The first – the animal model – we have already mentioned. Henry Miller, when he was Vice-Chancellor of Newcastle University, once defined mankind during a radio broadcast as 'just an enormously intelligent and intellectually agile animal'. Many experimental investigations in behavioural psychology performed in recent years have relied on that analogy between man and animals – usually rats!

Alongside the 'naked ape', however, another scientific model for man has emerged: that of the 'bionic machine'. Edmund Leach in his Reith Lectures back in the late sixties expressed this view candidly. He claimed that soon a complete description of man in biochemical terms would be available:

> There is no sharp break of continuity between what is human and what is mechanical. Today, when molecular

17

biologists are unravelling the genetic chemistry of all living things, and radio astronomers are deciphering the programme of an evolving cosmos, all the marvels of creation are seen to be mechanisms rather than mysteries. Since even the human brain is nothing more than an immensely complicated computer, it is no longer necessary to invoke metaphysics to explain how it works.

Self-consciousness and imagination

It is, of course, indisputable that man is biologically linked to the animal world and chemically linked to the inorganic universe, but it is equally clear that there are certain characteristics of human existence that do not really fit the animal or machine model very well. Psychologists are well aware of them and have given considerable attention to them. Just two of these we might consider are self-consciousness and imagination. The ability to formulate the question, 'Am I just an animal?' ironically indicates a capacity for self-transcendence that no animal seems to possess.

In one of his books Arthur Koestler points out that you can insert a platinum wire into the human skull and by stimulating it with electricity produce a physical response. When you ask the person why he did it he replies, 'I didn't do it – you made me do it.' Yet, of course, the same physical movement could have been made voluntarily. In the first case the neurones of the brain actuate from the outside. In the voluntary case, the same neurones of the brain actuate from inside. Then the person would say, 'Yes, I did it that time.'

How do we achieve that feat of self-conscious activity? Animals obey their instincts and machines their programming. Is there not something extraordinary about the way a person is able to use the personal pronoun 'I' and be the subject of his or her own actions? We can transcend our actions mentally and evaluate them, feeling proud or guilty, depending on how we feel about what we have done. Some people argue, of course, that self-consciousness is mechanical in origin. If we made a computer sufficiently complex, they say, with enough feedback loops, perhaps, it would start talking to us like Hal in Kubrick's *2001*, using the personal pronoun. But there is no empirical evidence for such a claim, and most scientists do not find the idea very convincing.

Then there is human imagination to consider. Much of what has been written about cave people is fanciful speculation, but one thing that does rest very firmly on observation is that these early people were artists. They painted for pleasure and they painted, of all things, animals. Isn't that interesting? Of course, the animal world produces many builders: thrushes make nests and bees construct honeycombs. But what made us architects? The animal world produces many singers, but what made us composers? The animal world produces many mimics, but what gave us our originality? Is that really just a difference of degree? Or is there not a discontinuity there?

These characteristics of self-consciousness and imagination are, as far as we can see, distinctively human, and they do not easily fit the animal and machine models.

It is surely legitimate to ask if there is an alternative model for human existence, and the book of Genesis insists that indeed there is. God said, 'Let us make man in our own image' (Gn. 1:26). Do you see what that means? According to the Bible, human beings cannot be properly understood by analogy to animals or machines. Human beings are qualitatively different from anything else in the whole of creation. It is possible to make full sense of a human being only by analogy to God. No other analogy, no other model, will do.

Now it is important once again to say that this does not mean we reject as rubbish the zoological or the biochemical understanding of man. There is all the difference in the world between formulating a correct description of something and claiming that that description is exhaustive. The problem with these machine and animal models is that they are not complete. The Bible agrees that man is chemically continuous with the rest of the inorganic world, because it says God made Adam 'from the dust of the ground' (Gn. 2:7). So it is no surprise that the urea which we produce is identical to the urea which can be synthesized in a laboratory. And the Bible agrees too that man is affiliated to the animal world, because Genesis says that 'man became a living being' (Gn. 2:7), a phrase which can apply to any form of animate life in Hebrew, including the animals.

Dignity

But the Bible insists that there is a third dimension to human existence. We may be dust, but we are not just dust. We have animal life but we also have a capacity for more than animal life. To say that human beings are made in the image of God, then, is not to contradict the scientific models, it is to complement them.

Equally, it is important to say that this does not necessarily contradict chemical or animal evolution as a mechanism for the creation of mankind. That question of mechanism is an interesting one, but it does not significantly affect this issue. G. K. Chesterton once commented:

> For a person who doesn't believe in a miracle, a slow miracle would be just as credible or incredible as a swift one. The Greek witch may have turned sailors into swine with a stroke of her wand, but to see a naval gentleman of our acquaintance looking a little bit more like a pig each day till he ended up with four trotters and a curly tail, would not be any more soothing.

The Bible does not say that some ancestral ape gradually evolved into a man. But even if that had happened, it would have taken a miracle, because a human being is different from an animal: humans are made in the image of God. Earlier in this

21

chapter we said that human self-consciousness does not easily fit the animal or machine model. This comes as no surprise, once we look at it from the biblical perspective. What do we find in Genesis 1:26 but God himself saying, 'Let us make man in our image'? What could be more self-conscious than that? Even one of the names for God in the Bible is 'I AM WHO I AM'. The ultimate truth behind the universe, claims the Bible, is not dead impersonal matter but living self-conscious spirit. And it is that fact that guarantees the significance of our self-consciousness. When a human being says, 'I am', he is not just demonstrating a certain degree of complexity in his brain, he is reflecting the divine image, the self-consciousness of the God in whose image he is made.

The distinctive human faculty of imagination also makes eminent sense on this biblical model. For what is God in Genesis 1, if he is not imaginative? He is the Creator. He makes the world itself by self-expression. God *said*, 'Let there be light' (Gn. 1:3). At each stage in his creative enterprise, just like the artist, he stands back with brush in hand and passes a value judgment on his work: 'It's good,' he says. So it is no surprise that human beings show the same kind of creative imagination and aesthetic awareness. Human art is meaningful, for in it we are rediscovering the appreciation which God expressed when he looked at what he had made and said, 'I like it.'

In both these areas, then – and there are many more we could discuss – the image-of-God model makes sense of things which do not fit the animal or machine model. The problem with both these models is that they are reductionist. They are not false, but they are not the whole truth. When you treat them as if they were the whole truth, you end up reducing human beings to something less than what they really are. For human beings are unique. Alone in the universe, the human race is God-like.

And that is what gives human beings their special dignity, value and importance. To treat human beings as if they were no more than animals or machines is to degrade them most grievously. In the phrase 'the image of God', once we have understood it, we find the theological roots of the Christian critique of all forms of dehumanization in our world today, whether it be racist or sexist prejudice, abortion on demand, indifference to the plight of the mentally handicapped, the trivialization of violence in the media, the exploitation of the poor, even the vexed question of capital punishment for murder. On all these issues Christians have a distinctive contribution to make because they have a distinctive conviction about the dignity of human beings. They see human beings not as mere animals, not as mere machines. The secular world runs into confusion over these moral issues because it is trying to solve them using an inadequate reductionist model for mankind. And the problem for secular thinkers does not stop there. They also have trouble understanding the rights and wrongs of human scientific advance.

3

Science in the Garden

Dominion

> God said, 'Let us make man in our
> image, in our likeness, and let them
> *rule* over the fish of the sea and the
> birds of the air, over the livestock, over
> all the earth . . .'
>
> (Gn. 1:26)

Human beings do have an extraordinary ability to
control the world around them. They have no
predatory teeth or claws, yet it is not the lion but the
human being who is the real king of the world.
When animals find their environment altered they
adapt by a process of evolutionary change, or they
become extinct. Human beings, on the other hand,
by virtue of their creative imagination, are able to
adapt themselves to their environment. Though
they have little body hair they can survive in Arctic
wastes as successfully as in equatorial heat. They
can even find ways to live on the inhospitable
surface of the moon. It is popular to attribute this to
man's intelligence, but Genesis insists that human
beings exercise this extraordinary dominion over

the world because they possess a special mandate from God himself. One of the reasons we were put on this earth was to be God's deputies, God's viceroys, God's stewards. This idea is developed in Genesis in two specific ways.

Adam was a worker

It is significant that the first time the word 'work' occurs in the Bible it is used of God. 'By the seventh day God had finished the work he had been doing' (Gn. 2:2). God's creational enterprise is work; and human beings work in imitation of him, as his divine image. 'The LORD God took the man and put him in the Garden of Eden to work it and take care of it' (Gn. 2:15). Here, then, is Adam's first taste of dominion. Work is not a curse, it is a consequence of his sovereign rule over the world, a dominion invested in him by God whose image he bears. Quite contrary to the ancient Greek view, much admired by the hippies in the sixties, and still not unknown on the campuses of universities, idleness is not the goal of human life.

We need to work to fulfil our destiny. This is something Karl Marx understood rather well. There is a work ethic in the Bible. Work is something good, something necessary to human beings. Whether it is paid or not, whether our twentieth century calls it 'work' or not, is neither here nor there. Human beings must work in order to demonstrate that they are human.

Adam was a scientist

The roots of human science are very clearly antici-
pated in the way God brings the animals and the
birds to Adam for him to name them. 'Now the
LORD God had formed out of the ground all the
beasts of the field and all the birds of the air. He
brought them to the man to see what he would
name them; and whatever the man called each
living creature, that was its name' (Gn. 2:19). God
did not name the animals, we're told; man named
them.

Now naming may seem a comparatively trivial
task, but in fact it's very significant in this context.
In Genesis 1, when God made the universe, it was
he who named things. By doing so he distin-
guished himself from nature. He made it clear that
he stands apart as a personal being distinct from
his creation and sovereign over it. And in the same
way, Adam, his image bearer, here testifies to the
same sense of personal distinctiveness. By naming
the animals he objectifies them, distinguishes
them from his own unique existence, and asserts
his sovereignty over them.

What we have here is the beginning of objectivity, the beginning of rational analysis – in short,
the beginning of science. All science is fundamentally about naming things. It classifies what
we observe. It studies a phenomenon (such as an
apple falling from a tree), notes its similarity to
another phenomenon (the orbit of the moon) and
gives both a common name (gravity). Identifying
phenomena which have something in common
and then putting them under the same label is a

descriptive exercise that is foundational to science. And that process of objectifying the world around us, analysing it and giving it names, has given us huge power. For it is an expression of the dominion which God has mandated his image bearer to exert over the world.

This has great relevance to the whole debate about the New Age movement, especially in its connections with the Green movement. One of the things which Eastern religion does is to impart a superstitious reverence for nature which inhibits our willingness to control our environment. Hinduism teaches that there are no ultimate distinctions in the universe; everything is a manifestation of one cosmic spirit; everything is divine. And the result of that, of course, is that people go hungry rather than kill the rats or the cows that eat the corn. Science can never grow out of that kind of pantheistic worldview. From an Eastern mystical point of view, it would be essentially irreligious to name things. To distinguish yourself from other things and stand over against them, to objectify them and analyse them, is to deny the essential oneness of everything. According to Eastern religion, such science is unspiritual and impious. This is an extraordinary irony, of course. The science which so many people even today still seem to regard as the great enemy of the Bible could, in fact, never have developed if the Bible had not provided us with its theistic understanding of the world and of our special human relationship to it.

Some in the Green lobby would want to argue that it would have been a very good thing if

science had not developed. They point to the ecological catastrophes which the undisciplined use of
science is producing. Wouldn't it be better, they
say, if we had a less superior, more mystical, more
reverential attitude towards nature? Why not call
nature Gaia and attribute to it some sort of personal existence, some kind of feminine con-
sciousness, like 'Mother Nature', which we must
not violate? Then we wouldn't abuse nature so,
would we? But their criticisms are ill judged.
Science and technology in the twentieth century
have become such dreadful agents of destruction
not because human beings were wrong to feel
themselves monarchs of the universe, but because
their sense of dominion has become divorced from
something which, according to Genesis, must
invariably go with it – that is, responsibility.

4

The great big 'but'

> The LORD God commanded the man,
> 'You are free to eat from any tree in
> the garden; but you must not eat from
> the tree of the knowledge of good and
> evil, for when you eat of it you will
> surely die.'
>
> (Gn. 2:16–17)

Life was easy in the Garden of Eden. Everything the human race needed was laid on. We read that there were trees pleasing to the eye – that is, things to satisfy man's aesthetic awareness; there were trees good for food, to meet his nutritional needs; and most interesting of all, there was the tree of life. This mysterious symbol (or was it a real tree?) clearly stands for the satisfaction of the spiritual aspirations of man's personality, of his appetite for immortality. God wanted human beings to enjoy all this. 'You are free to eat from any tree,' he said – a huge orbit of unfettered liberty.

There are some, of course, who seem to think that austerity is more spiritual than pleasure. In fact, quite early on the Christian church was invaded by an anti-materialist asceticism derived from Platonic philosophy, claiming that you could purify the soul by denying the body. There are residual evidences of this even today in things like the celibacy of the Roman Catholic priesthood and the voluntary poverty of some monastic orders. You find similar, if less institutionalized, vestiges of asceticism among Protestant Christians too. It is far from unusual in counselling people from a very strict puritanical background to discover that they think they are being moral when in fact they are simply being uncomfortable. 'It must be wicked,' they say to themselves, 'I enjoyed it too much.'

In more general terms, it is this sort of attitude which leads some Christians to think that it is more spiritual to be a missionary than a banker, or to be a vicar than an engineer. It is what makes them suspicious about getting involved with the creation of wealth or prosperity and leads them to think that it is holier to eat lentils than to eat steak, or to ride a bicycle than to drive a car. None of this is true. All asceticism and anti-materialism of this sort betrays a deficient doctrine of creation. Paul puts it very clearly to Timothy when he says, 'Everything God created is good, and nothing is to be rejected if it is received with thanksgiving' (1 Tim. 4:4).

Conditional freedom

Adam and Eve were free in Eden to explore the material world and to enjoy it. Indeed, they were not even told to stay in the Garden; there was the possibility of adventure too, because we read of fascinating new lands to explore, new mineral resources to discover, gold and onyx and pearls (Gn. 2:12). In this great orbit of permission God placed only one restriction, one 'but': 'but you must not eat from the tree of the knowledge of good and evil' (Gn. 2:17). People have tried to identify exactly what the eating of this tree signified. Sometimes it has been suggested that there was a sexual connotation. Others say it represents some sphere of prohibited knowledge like the occult. But the truth is that we are not told, because the tree is there simply to indicate that the freedom God gives to human beings must be a conditional freedom. It is liberty under law. They are free to do as they *ought*. They are not free to do as they *want*. Unconditional liberty is not available to human beings.

We rule, but our dominion is a stewardship, limited by the sovereignty of the God who delegates it to us. So there has to be a 'but'. And the reason our world is in a mess is that we human beings resented the 'but'. We were not content with the humble dignity of being made in the image of God. In our arrogance we grasped at deity itself. We wanted no inhibiting 'buts' limiting our freedom of action. We wanted moral autonomy, we wanted to rule not only the world but ourselves. And there lies the root of our ecological crises. There is the source of our economic recessions. There is the source of all our frustrated longings for Utopia. We do not want to be commanded.

God said, 'You are free, *but* . . . .' Man has replied, 'No, I'm free – no "buts"!' People sometimes talk about the importance of human free will. But the truth is that it is the shame of

31

humanity that we live as if we could choose 'freely' outside the will of God. The freedom God offers us is the privilege of voluntary obedience. We are free so long as we agree with God and stay within the circle of permission which he defines for us. If we want to find fulfilment and satisfaction, we must learn to accept that accountability; we must let God tell us what is right and wrong and refuse to try to make up the rules ourselves. He has huge things for us to enjoy. He has work for us to do. But we will miss it all unless we bow our proud heads and accept his authority over our lives.

This responsibility is what marks us out from animals, perhaps more than anything else. Like God himself, we have the power to choose. God has not made us animals which just obey instinct or computers which just follow programmes. He has made us moral agents, and this is why we may live either in paradise or in hell.

5

We need us

Relationship

> The LORD God said, 'It is not good for
> the man to be alone. I will make a
> helper suitable for him.'
>
> (Gn. 2:18)

This is fascinating. God has examined every corner
of the world and pronounced it 'good'. Now
suddenly we find a different verdict. Something is
not good. Mankind is lacking something – something which no tree in the Garden can provide. In
fact it is not a something but a someone.

Back in Genesis 1 we encounter a rather
unexpected use of the plural pronoun for God:
'God said, "Let *us* make man in *our* image"' (v.
26). That may be simply a Hebrew idiom to
indicate the power of God, rather like the royal
'we' of which Queen Victoria was so fond. And we
could be satisfied with that explanation, I think, if
it were not for the fact that precisely the same
swing between singular and plural is used of the
image of God. 'So God created *man* in his own
image, in the image of God he created *him*

(singular); *male* and *female* he created *them* (plural)'
(Gn. 1:27). There is surely an implication there that
to image God adequately there had to be more
than one person; that male and female *together* are
the image of God. Indeed, if we have any doubt on
that point, it is conclusively answered a few chapters later: 'When God created man, he made him in
the likeness of God. He created them male and
female; at the time they were created, he blessed
them and called them "man"' (Gn. 5:1–2). This
observation is of enormous relevance to the whole
feminist debate. The image of God does not consist
in the male alone, but in male and female together.
Long ago, Saint Augustine defended the doctrine
of the Trinity by suggesting that if God was love,
then from all eternity he must have had some*one* to
love, for love can exist only in the context of interpersonal relationships. Hence the Trinity, he
argued.

It takes two to be glad

Are we speculating too far if we say that God's
sensitivity to Adam's loneliness is due precisely to
that structure of interpersonal relationships within
God's own nature? It is not good for man to be
alone, for man is made in the image of God, and
God is not alone. The image of God is not fully
reflected till God has taken man and divided him,
so that man, like God, is able to love another
person.

The implications of this go far. It is the root of
the Bible's understanding of marriage. 'For this
reason a man will leave his father and mother and

be united to his wife, and they will become one flesh' (Gn. 2:24). Of course, the Bible isn't negative about the single life. It recognizes celibacy as a vocation to which some are called. The apostle Paul even calls being single a gift, or literally a *charisma*. If people are tempted to think that the Bible despises the unmarried state, they have only to consider the virginity of Jesus to find themselves put straight. There are unique opportunities and blessings in being single – of that the Bible is certain. But the Bible is equally adamant that singleness is unusual. It is not the norm, because in general it is not good for us to be alone. We are social creatures; to be totally fulfilled, most of us need the companionship and the security of a marriage partner. As someone has said, you can be sad on your own; it takes two to be glad.

There was a time when the church, in its teaching on marriage, laid great emphasis on the importance of children. Of course, it is obvious that one of the major reasons for the social importance of marriage is the environment it provides for the nurture of the next generation. There's no way state nurseries will ever do a better job. But it was unfortunate that the church laid so much stress on procreation as the purpose of marriage, because that does not seem to be the primary thrust of the book of Genesis. God does not say, 'It is not good for man to be childless'; he says, 'It is not good for man to be alone' (Gn. 2:18). Marriage, according to the Bible, is complete and fulfilled even without children. The primary relationship is that between husband and wife.

In a sense it is a mistake to speak of 'Christian

marriage', because clearly here marriage belongs to the whole of mankind, not just the church. It is an inescapable part of our human nature as God has created us. Some sociologists, of course, would dispute that. For them, marriage is just a particular phase in social evolution. Once it ceases to have survival value it will become extinct, like the environmentally outdated dinosaur. Some would even argue that we are on the verge of that transition now. Marriage as an institution is soon going to break down completely and wither away. But the Bible insists that it will not be so. Marriage is built into human beings. We can never evolve beyond the need for it.

And there is plenty of evidence for that biblical claim. Several societies have tried to extinguish the family and marriage. One thinks of the early Soviets in the USSR, or some of the kibbutzim in Israel. All these experiments have failed. Try to destroy the bond of marriage, and it will simply reassert itself. No matter how easy you make divorce, no matter how relaxed you are about sexual promiscuity, people will always want that special pair bond. Marriage is not a piece of learned behaviour; it is not a cultural adaptation; it is a creation norm. Genesis says, 'For this reason [*i.e.* because man was made like this] a man will leave his father and mother and be united to his wife' (Gn. 2:24). It is a permanent, universal institution in human society. And that is why as Christians we must be so concerned about the family today. If we allow it to be attacked our whole society will suffer pain. This complex of relationships which we call the family is not some accident of social evolution; it is part of our image of God. God himself exists in a complex of relationships, and our families are meant to reflect the same sort of love that binds the Godhead.

'The man and his wife were both naked and they felt no shame' (Gn. 2:25). Suspicion could not torment this relationship; lust could not brutalize it; self-consciousness could not artificialize it. Genesis 2 ends with a picture of human beings in total harmony with each other, with their world and with their God. And yet there is a pathos here. For verse 25 is in the past tense. The man and his wife *were* both naked and felt no shame.

Dignity, dominion, responsibility, relationship. The image of God was as yet unmarred, but it was an image that was going to be disastrously broken.

Part two

Fall

6

The twilight of Utopia

There is a hymn which you will not find in many modern hymnbooks. It goes like this:

> These things shall be, a loftier race
> Than e'er the world hath known shall
>   rise,
> With flame of freedom in their souls
> And light of knowledge in their eyes.
>
> They shall be gentle, brave and strong
> To spill no drop of blood but dare
> All that may plant man's lordship on
> The earth and fire and sea and air.
>
> New arts shall bloom of loftier mould
> And mightier music thrill the skies
> And every life shall be a song
> When all the earth is paradise.

Why don't they write hymns like that nowadays? I suppose it's because we don't believe in them any longer. We have lost confidence in Utopia. We stand on the threshold of a new millennium, but our courage is failing us. An atmosphere of disillusionment is in the air. It has been in the air for quite a few years now. H. G Wells was an enthusiastic mouthpiece of humanistic optimism in the first half of this century. In 1937 he wrote:

> Can we doubt that presently our race will more than realize our boldest imaginations; that it will achieve unity and peace; that it will live in a world made more splendid and lovely than any palace or garden that we know; going on from strength to strength in ever widening circles of adventure and achievement? What man has done, the little triumphs of his present state, form but the prelude to the things that man has yet to do.

It took only two years to shatter that dream for Wells. Confronted by the outbreak of World War 2, he sang a completely different tune in 1939. He wrote:

> In spite of all my dispositions to a brave-looking optimism, I perceive that the universe is now bored with man and is turning a hard face to him. I see him being carried less and less intelligently and more and more rapidly along the stream of fate to degradation, suffering and death. The spectacle of evil in this world has come near to breaking my spirit altogether. *Homo sapiens*, as he has

been pleased to call himself, is played out.

It would be nice to be able to say that this was just depression, born of the impact of war on a very sensitive intellectual. But Wells' pessimism has been echoed by many other seminal thinkers of the second half of our century. What has happened to that vision of 'a loftier race'? It lies shattered, a Utopian dream that few now believe in. Human beings have lost confidence in themselves. It is not that the problems confronting us at the end of the century cannot be solved. The question that haunts us, undermining the optimism that was once so characteristic of our century, is whether human beings are responsible enough, self-disciplined enough, unselfish enough, just plain good enough to implement those solutions.

Original sin

Professor Joad was an agnostic for many years and a convinced socialist. He believed passionately in the ability of man to control his own destiny. But slowly that conviction was weakened, just as in the case of H. G. Wells. Reality just did not correspond to Joad's dreams. And eventually he put his finger on the problem. In a book entitled *The Recovery of Belief* he wrote this in 1952:

We on the left were always being disappointed. Disappointed by the refusal of people to be reasonable, by the subservience of intellect to emotion, by the failure of true socialism to arrive, by the behaviour of nations and politicians, by the masses' preference of Hollywood to Shakespeare, of Sinatra to Beethoven. Above all, we are disappointed by the recurrent fact of war. The reason for our disappointment is that we have rejected the doctrine of original sin.

The optimism of humanists and of early socialists all hinged on the belief that man was basically good. True, there were vestiges of his animal origins apparent in his personality, but evolution was systematically eliminating such defects. Man was getting better and better all the time. Nothing could halt his progress towards God-like perfection and earthly paradise. But unfortunately the evidence does not match that optimism. Victor Firkiss in a more recent book entitled *Technological Man* says:

Modern man is very far from slaying the beast within. Why should we assume that the man of the future will be a completely new creature? What if the man of the twenty-first century combined the animal irrationality of early man with the calculated greed and power lust of industrial man while possessing the

God-like power of technological
man? This would be the ultimate
horror.

Paradise lost

So that loss of hope which Wells experienced and
which Joad analysed has become reflected in the
writings of more and more recent thinkers. The
'loftier race' that we were certain would arise is
now revealed to be a myth. Indeed, this is the real
irony of the failure of Marxism in Eastern Europe
and the USSR. It did not fail because capitalism is
a morally superior system. Transparently it is not.
No, Marxism failed because, where capitalism
exploits the fundamental selfishness and greed of
human beings, Marxism makes no allowance for
it at all. It assumes that people are going to be
unselfish, when they simply are not.

In his book *The Wealth of Nations* Adam Smith
said: 'It is not from the benevolence of the butcher
or the baker we expect our daily bread, but from
their regard for their own self-interest.' In other
words, if you are going to build an economic system, you had better be realistic about sin, said
Adam Smith. He was a vicar. He knew about
such things. The reason Utopian socialism fails is
because it neglects this warp in human nature
which constantly frustrates our attempts to build
a better, fairer, classless society. And yet isn't it
true that in some haunting way that longing for a
better world, that longing for some more optimistic perspective on the future, tantalizes the
human race? What is this longing? Is it just a

dream of Utopia which people need to entertain in order to overcome their despair?

Now the Bible would say that it is something more than that. The Bible would say that this haunting longing for a better world is a memory; a racial memory of a paradise we have lost.

7

Trap-door to death

> The serpent was more crafty than any
> of the wild animals the Lᴏʀᴅ God had
> made. He said to the woman, 'Did
> God really say you must not eat from
> any tree in the garden?'
>
> (Gn. 3:1)

When we get to Genesis 2:4, Bible history begins in
the sense that now we are reading something
which claims to draw on human memory for its
source. But that does not mean necessarily that
figurative language could not have been employed
in recounting these primeval events. It is possible
that choices and influences that were originally
internal to the minds of Adam and Eve could have
been given substance in the shape of trees and a
serpent in order to make the telling of the story
easier. However, there is no evidence to suggest
that the writer does not intend us to understand
this narrative quite literally.

It is true that animals do not usually speak, and
there is no reason to believe that the situation in
the Garden of Eden was any different in this
respect. The serpent's speech was supernatural

even in the context of paradise. Later passages in the Bible make it clear that the serpent was acting as the mouthpiece of demonic intelligence here. Satan, it seems, found the natural stealth and cunning with which the Creator had equipped the snake a suitable vehicle for his own insidious campaign.

Doubt

'Did God really say, "You must not eat from any tree in the garden"?' (Gn. 3:1). Do you notice the overstatement there: 'any tree'? Satan knew perfectly well that the extent of God's prohibition was tiny in comparison with the huge orbit of permission which he had given to man. But Satan's aim is to sow seeds of rebellion. And what better way than to portray God as a great spoilsport, the mean-minded parent who always wants to say no? He uses the same ploy today to undermine our willingness to accept the limitations which God places on our actions. 'Oh, Christianity,' he says. 'All those "thou shalt nots", those rules and regulations. So dull and inhibiting.'

The woman in her initial response seems secure. She will correct this foolish animal's misinformation. But it is never safe to open a conversation with the devil, no matter how well informed or how well intentioned you may be. You are unlikely to convert him, and he is very likely to corrupt you. Already, without her being aware of it in the least, Satan has persuaded Eve that God's commandments are a subject for human debate and discussion. She says to the serpent, 'We may eat fruit from the trees in the garden, but God did say, "You must not eat fruit from the tree that is in the middle of the garden, and you must not touch it, or you will die"' (Gn. 3:2–3). Is there just a tinge of petulant resentment there? After all, God has not actually said they should not *touch* it. Was the woman perhaps exaggerating the strictness of the command, as a sulky child sometimes does? 'Oh, you never let me go out in the evenings,' when actually it is the 'in by eleven' rule that he or she is complaining about.

The devil is very quick to pursue his advantage. 'You will not surely die,' he says to the woman. 'God knows that when you eat of it your eyes will be opened' (Gn. 3:4–5). So from suggesting that the command is unkind and small-minded, he proceeds now to a rank denial of the sincerity of the sanction: 'You will not die.' This is a direct contradiction of what God had said, an explicit challenge to God's truthfulness and authority. It is the lie with which Satan has continued to dupe human beings into a false sense of security ever since. 'You can get away with it,' he says. 'God's threat is empty. All this talk about judgment? Hell, fire and brimstone? It's just scaremongering, sabre-rattling. As if God could possibly do anything so nasty to you!'

So he denies both the goodness and severity of God in a single breath, first complaining of the cruelty of God in making the commandment and then assuring us that he could not possibly be so cruel as to condemn us for breaking it. Here is Satan's first tactic, to sow seeds of doubt about the trustworthiness of God and his word.

Pride

'God knows that when you eat of it your eyes will be opened, and you will be like God, knowing good and evil' (Gn. 3:5). In other words, 'You are capable of being much greater than you are. God is just bluffing when he says no, to keep you under his thumb. He wants you to be dependent on him, crawling to him, but you can do without him. Assert your will; make your own choice. Humility is a vice; where's your self-respect? Break out of this servile submission. Reject his authoritarian tyranny over your life. Be free. Be independent. Be your own God!'

So arises the fiendish logic of all revolution: that anarchy somehow possesses more dignity than obedience; that self-assertion is more admirable than self-abasement; that rebels are more heroic than servants; that people who break rules are somehow more authentically human than those who keep them. Marx and Sartre have said it at greater length, but not to greater effect. Indeed, this is the Promethean arrogance that underlies all humanism. Dissatisfied with the humble dignity of being made in the image of their Creator, humanists must grasp at deity itself. Their attitude is, 'Glory to man in the highest! He is the master of things!'

Desire

'When the woman saw that the fruit of the tree was good for food and pleasing to the eye, and also desirable for gaining wisdom, she took some and ate it. She also gave some to her husband, who was with her, and he ate it' (Gn 3:6). Notice the threefold appeal to the physical, aesthetic and intellectual appetites. We often think of lust as if it were exclusively a bodily passion. That is not so. The focus of lust varies with personality and with gift. It is true, there are some men who would sell their souls to possess a woman; but there are some men who would sell their souls to own a painting; and there are some men who would sell their souls to solve an equation. A man may fall victim to desire in any field. In fact, what we have here is an example of the hedonistic self-indulgence which is so peculiarily characteristic of our age. If I find something pleasurable, if I find something satisfying, if I find something enriching, then it has to be OK for me to have it. Self-denial can never be right. This is the attitude of much cheap-jack psychotherapy today. This is the philosophy of *Playboy* magazine. Anything that inhibits my free expression, anything that places a check on my behaviour, anything that stops me experiencing what I want to experience, must be wrong. Self-fulfilment is the ultimate goal of human existence.

Weakness

'She took some and ate it. She also gave some to her husband, who was with her, and he ate it' (Gn. 3:6). The easiest way of eliminating desire is to surrender to it. Whatever the subtle appeals of Satan, they were not irresistible. The woman did not have to talk to him. The serpent was, after all, an inferior creature that she was supposed to

51

tame, yet she soaked up its instruction like a sponge. The woman did not have to take from the tree herself. The strength was there to say no if she had exerted it. And the man did not have to accept his wife's seduction. No doubt evil is always easier when it comes to us clothed in sexual attraction. But Adam abdicated his responsibility in the marriage bond. Instead of leading he followed. So from beginning to end it was a surrender without a fight, a pathetic capitulation: doubt, pride, desire, and now not even a shadow of resistance.

So often sin invades our lives in just such a way. 'You will enjoy it,' says Satan. 'Yes, I will,' we reply. 'You deserve it,' says Satan. 'Yes, I do,' we reply. 'You can get away with it,' says Satan. 'Yes, I can,' we reply. 'It's a ridiculous rule anyway,' says Satan. 'So it is,' we reply. So we just give in. God made us monarchs of the universe, but we behave like jellyfish, like moral invertebrates. 'The flesh is weak,' said Jesus. He never spoke a truer word. When sin invades our lives, this is how it always comes. What forbidden fruits have we plucked? Whatever they are, you can be sure that doubt, pride, desire and weakness were the things which made us vulnerable.

8

The great collapse

> Then the eyes of both of them were
> opened, and they realised that they
> were naked; so they sewed fig leaves
> together and made coverings for
> themselves.
>
> (Gn. 3:7)

Shame

We might have expected that some divine thun-
derbolt would fall upon the guilty pair. But in fact,
shame was the first and most immediate consequence. Shame would be followed by fear,
excuses and finally judgment. There was a kind of
warped veracity in the serpent's claim. Rebellion
against God has changed their perception of the
world. 'To the pure, all things are pure,' says Paul,
'but to those who are corrupted ... nothing is
pure' (Tit. 1:15). Suddenly all kinds of new possi-
bilities flood into their imaginations. Now that
they have chosen to throw off the Creator's order
and establish their own norms of behaviour, ideas
arise in their minds that make them blush. The
discovery of sin introduces a new tension into their

relationship, therefore: suspicion, distrust, self-consciousness, embarrassment. They can no longer be completely open with each other. They no longer completely trust each other. They veil their bodies in a pathetic attempt to conceal their thoughts. They set up psychological defences against each other. Suddenly they find they need privacy.

Fear

'Then the man and his wife heard the sound of the LORD God as he was walking in the garden in the cool of the day, and they hid from the LORD God among the trees of the garden. But the LORD God called to the man, "Where are you?" He answered, "I heard you in the garden, and I was afraid because I was naked; so I hid"' (Gn. 3:8–10). Not only do they hide from each other, but they feel a desperate need to hide from God too. Not just because of the humiliation they feel, but because they are afraid. Are these the ones who wanted to be God? More like naughty children, they are crouched in the broom-cupboard. 'What will he do when he finds out?' they say to each other. Did they really think they could escape the limitations of their human nature? An elephant cannot fly; he has no wings. He is not meant to fly. He was not made to fly. And a human being cannot play at being God. We were not designed for that role. We may in our impudence choose to defy God's will, but it is a futile defiance. We wave our fists at him in vain, because he remains the King. There is no way we can divest him of his omnipotence; no way we can reverse the arrow of moral responsibility. We are his creation, and it is utterly pointless to try to evade the consequences of our creatureliness. And yet that is so often what we seek to do.

Some of us, perhaps, in our arrogance, imagine ourselves arraigning God before our human tribunal on the last day and giving him a bit of our mind. We will indict him with all our complaints about his maladministration and injustice. But it's all fantasy, isn't it? We know that if we should ever meet God it would not be like that at all. It is we who would cringe terrified, not he. It is we who would have to give an explanation of ourselves, not he. So when we are in a more realistic frame of mind what we try to do instead is keep him at arm's length. Like Adam and Eve, to flee his inexorable advance we hide: perhaps in our activities, perhaps in our books, perhaps in our relationships – any bush will do. 'They called to the mountains and the rocks, "Fall on us and hide us from the face of him who sits on the throne"' (Rev. 6:16). But there is no mountain big enough to shield us from the face of our Maker.

Excuses

'He said, "Who told you that you were naked? Have you eaten from the tree that I commanded you not to eat from?" The man said, "The woman you put here with me – she gave me some fruit from the tree, and I ate it"' (Gn. 3:11–12). Here is the most typical human response to sin. We think to escape our shame and our fear by passing the buck. Adam blamed Eve, Eve blamed the serpent and the serpent hadn't got a leg to stand on.

Long books have been written about the origin of evil. It is a problem, we are told. How did evil invade a world that was passed wholly good by God's own verdict in the beginning? Where did this strange evil come from? Two answers have been chiefly proposed, and you catch a glimpse of both of them in this dialogue. One answer is that of monism, which says that both good and evil originate in the one God. That is Adam's line. 'The woman you put here with me . . .' (Gn. 3:12). In other words, 'It's your fault, God. If there's a blunder here, you initiated it.'

The other answer that is often proposed is dualism. Dualism sets up two equal and opposite powers in the universe – God and the devil. It attributes all the good things to God and all the evil things to the devil. That is Eve's line. 'The serpent deceived me,' she says (Gn. 3:13).

The fact is, the Bible rejects both of these alternative solutions. On the one hand, it insists that God is not the author of sin; he is utterly opposed to it. So monism is excluded. On the other hand, the Bible refuses to make Satan equal with God. The serpent is explicitly stated to be one of the creatures which God made, which he originally pronounced good. So what is the answer, then, to this mystery of the origin of evil? The truth is, the Bible never gives us one. Perhaps that is because in the Bible's view it is an illegitimate question. We human beings are interested in the origin of evil only because we are looking for an excuse, as Adam and Eve were. We want to say, 'There, that's why I did it. It's my genes, it's my parents, it's the social system. It's that woman. It's that devil.' We want to rationalize our sin so that we can evade its guilt.

The Bible will not allow us to do that. Evil cannot be explained. It lies outside the range of causality and logic. It is an essentially irrational intrusion into God's world. There was no valid reason for man's sin – that is the whole point. It was an act of culpable folly. There may have been mitigating circumstances; there may have been others implicated in the crime. But that serves only to modify the penalty; it cannot reverse the verdict. What Genesis wants us to realize is that mankind is guilty. The buck stops here. We should not look around for some source for this strange evil that has invaded us so cruelly. The only valid response to our sin is confession. We need to say, 'I did it. It began with me. I am the origin of this evil.' But confession is humiliating, and we prefer to keep our self-respect by looking for excuses – excuses that do not exist. Deep in our hearts we know that nothing makes us sin, that we are not the victims of compulsion. We choose, and because we choose, we are responsible.

Judgment

God said to Adam, 'Because you listened to your wife and ate from the tree about which I commanded you, 'You must not eat of it,'' Cursed is the ground because of you; through painful toil you will eat of it all the days of your life. It will produce thorns and thistles for you, and you will eat the plants of the field. By the sweat of your brow you will eat your food until you return to the ground, since from it you were taken; for dust you are and to dust you will return' (Gn. 3:17–19). There is much that could detain us for a long while in the judicial penalties that God imposes here upon the man and the woman. We can do little more than mention the main components of God's judgment.

There is a disturbance in human relationships: 'Your desire will be for your husband, and he will rule over you' (Gn. 3:16). So the harmony and the equality that had characterized their relationship at first would now be distorted by the demands of sexual passion and by the tyranny of physical strength.

A disturbance too in the created order: 'It will produce thorns and thistles for you' (Gn. 3:18). That control over nature which the human race would have enjoyed is forfeited. Ecological balance will now prove elusive. The elements will threaten mankind's very existence, causing anxiety and toil.

Suffering too enters the world: 'I will greatly increase your pains in childbearing' (Gn. 3:16); 'through painful toil you will eat of it all the days of your life' (Gn. 3:17). Significantly, it is childbirth and daily labour, those things which ought to have brought the greatest fulfilment to men and women, which are now marred by pain.

But pain is only the prelude to death: 'for dust you are and to dust you will return' (Gn. 3:19). Originally the possibility of immortality had been available to Adam in Eden; there had been no prohibition regarding the tree of life. But now we read that 'a flaming sword' would guard the way to it (Gn. 3:24). All man's achievements, no matter how noble, would end in the futility of the grave.

We have a word in our twentieth century that expresses much of our human frustration. It is the word 'alienation'. Here is the source of it. Alienation within marriage, alienation within work, but supremely alienation from God: 'the LORD God banished him from the Garden of Eden to work the ground from which he had been taken' (Gn. 3:23). Of course, Adam did not leave God behind in Eden, but he certainly did forfeit the privilege of walking with God without shame and without fear. And the tragedy is that he forfeited it not only for himself but for all his posterity. The innocence he lost could never be recovered. Sin had entered the world. The rebellion had begun and now Adam's children would be born outside Eden.

9

East of Eden

We have not got the space to examine the subsequent chapters of Genesis in detail. But suffice it to say that they chronicle the way in which sin, the vicious virus which had infected the human race, brought death and misery in its wake to everybody and to everything.

Chapter 4, for instance, recounts the story of Cain and Abel. It startles us with the news that the first baby to be born turned out to be a murderer. And the divine curse is reinforced as a result: 'Today you are driving me from the land, and I will be hidden from your presence; I will be a restless wanderer on the earth, and whoever finds me will kill me' (Gn. 4:14). And do you notice how Cain tries to cope with this alienated existence of his, 'east of Eden' (Gn. 4:16)? Verse 17 says he built a city. In the estimation of the author of Genesis, there is something sinister about man's ambition to urbanize his environment. God gave us a garden. Now severed from God, we try to build our own alternative. Perhaps there is a depth we don't realize in that modern phrase, 'the concrete jungle'. Perhaps the city is our botched version of Eden. God is too obvious in nature. We must exclude his disturbing testimony with bricks and mortar. In our hostility to God we must try to surround ourselves with the artefacts of our own human creation. Out of the city of Cain, a culture emerged. In chapter 4 we read of music and metal-craft and farming. The image of God has not been completely lost. Man's creative imagination is still there. But it is a Godless culture that results now, an alienated culture. The city of Cain is the secular city, the place where men hide to forget God, and consequently the place where moral standards inevitably decay. In verse 19 the beginning of poly-gamy is noted almost in passing. And in verses 23–24 Lamech celebrates his deed of savagery: 'I have killed a man for wounding me, a young man for injuring me. If Cain is avenged seven times, then Lamech seventy-seven times.' Cain's crime seems tame by comparison. He at least denied his misdeed, but Lamech here boasts of his. Cain at least feared the vengeance of God. Lamech seems utterly contemptuous of divine retribution. This is the world Cain has built, east of Eden, a world where family life deteriorates and where violence escalates. Most characteristic of all, it is a world of universal death.

'And then he died'

Cast your eye down the long genealogy which comprises Genesis 5. You will find there one phrase that keeps on repeating like an ominous drumbeat at the end of each paragraph: 'and then he died ... and then he died ... and then he died'. The human race is multiplying as God said it would, but multiplying only to face the bitter grief and despair of death. 'When you eat of it you will surely die' (Gn. 2:17).

Chapter 6 begins with a poignant description of how God was feeling about this appalling ruin of his beautiful world: 'The LORD saw how great man's wickedness on the earth had become, and that every inclination of the thoughts of his heart was only evil all the time' (Gn. 6:5). The first time God looked at the world he saw it was good. Now he looks again and his verdict is totally different. It is hard to imagine a more uncompromising expression of the depth of God's horror at the magnitude of man's moral depravity. The universality of it: 'every inclination'. The inveteracy of it: 'only evil all the time'. The penetration of it: 'the thoughts of his heart'. This is not, then, the record of crimes performed by a small minority of mankind. This is a society in which everybody is motivated by evil, in which every construct of the human imagination is moulded by wickedness. This is a culture which seems quite literally beyond redemption. The moral decay which foolish Adam had introduced, which murderous Cain had confirmed, has now developed into a horrendous epidemic of vice.

The agony of God

Notice God's response to this appalling spectacle of evil: 'The LORD was grieved that he had made man on the earth, and his heart was filled with pain' (Gn. 6:6). This is technically called an anthropomorphism. God is being spoken of as if he shared human emotions. As if ... ? What makes us so sure he does not share our emotions? It is true that nothing happens outside God's sovereign will, but that does not mean that he approves of everything he permits. God never makes mistakes, but that does not mean that he never has regrets. God is never taken by surprise, but that does not mean that he can never be disappointed. God can never be thwarted, but that does not mean that he can never be hurt.

The cross is there in time and history to prove to us that our sins, though they cannot defeat God, nevertheless tear the heart of God apart with suffering. God is grieved at sin. This is no naive anthropomorphism; it is a profound insight into the emotional life of God. Divine judgment is no mechanical, cold-blooded vengeance pursuing man as the relentless hounds do a fox. No, God agonizes before he judges, as Jesus wept over Jerusalem. Make no mistake about it, as the rain began to fall on that corrupt antediluvian world, the tears of God were mingled with it. And we dare not read the awful words that follow, except in the context of that grief-stricken divine countenance: 'So the LORD said, "I will wipe mankind, whom I have created, off from the face of the earth"' (Gn. 6:7). 'Perhaps,' God almost seems to speculate, 'eugenics is the answer. Let's eradicate this morally corrupt human stock and start again with just a single family, the one family on earth I'm really pleased with.' Genesis tells us that 'Noah found favour in the eyes of the LORD' (Gn. 6:8). 'I will establish my covenant with you,' says God, 'and you will enter the ark' (Gn. 6:18).

Surely now, with a fresh start, paradise will be

regained. And indeed, after the flood, Genesis 9 does begin on a very hopeful note, full of optimistic possibility. Noah, like a second Adam, steps out of the ark into the pristine purity of a new world from which every trace of wickedness has been judicially purged. The rainbow sign of the peace treaty between God and man embraces the horizon. Surely now at last man will find his way back to the Garden of Eden, and the paradise which he had so foolishly forfeited will be regained. The creation mandate is reaffirmed in Genesis 9:1. God blesses Noah and his sons, saying to them, 'Be fruitful and increase in number and fill the earth,' just as he had said to Adam.

The same old story

Yet within a few verses all our fond hopes are smashed to pieces: 'Noah, a man of the soil, proceeded to plant a vineyard. When he drank some of its wine, he became drunk and lay uncovered inside his tent' (Gn. 9:20). He did not build a city as Cain had done, but the message of continuing failure is unmistakable. It is possible, of course, to draw moralizing conclusions about alcohol abuse here. Certainly there have been countless others who since Noah have fallen victim to strong drink, but that really misses the entire point. What we have here is an ironic parallel to the tragic story with which Genesis begins. Adam falls by eating the fruit of the tree, Noah by drinking the fruit of the vine. Adam discovers the treachery of the serpent, Noah discovers the treachery of the grape. Both are humiliated by the exposure of their nakedness, and both end up with the harmony of a perfect world spoiled and dislocated by a curse (Gn. 9:24).

The difference is that in Noah's case God takes no direct hand in the proceedings at all. Adam ate of the tree which God had planted; Noah eats of his own tree. Adam's nakedness was discovered by God's initiative; Noah's by his own children. Adam's judgment was pronounced by God; Noah delivers his own curse. For what we have here is not a second fall. It is that old fall rearing its ugly head again like some phoenix out of the ashes of judgment. The flood has not exorcized the demon in man. Sin is still there. Its virus is alive and kicking, embedded in the very structure of human personality and human relationships.

God had promised that he would not curse the world again. He didn't need to. For it is clear now that left to themselves, fallen mankind will quickly curse the world for him. Sin is not a single gene to be bred out of the human race by careful selection. It is a corruption that permeates every aspect of every personality. No-one is immune, not even Noah. This individual whom God calls 'righteous' has the same root of self-indulgence, the same inclination to abuse God's good creation as Adam had. And among his sons there is the identical mixture of honour and dishonour that led to the rivalry between Cain and Abel. So Genesis 9, which begins with bright optimism, ends with the same old story of brothers divided by a curse. The flood had been a judgment against sin, but it was not a remedy. Like radical surgery, it had reduced the tumour, but it had not eradicated its malignancy; the symptoms were still there, unmistakably sinister.

10

The ultimate horror

Now the whole world had one language and a common speech. As men moved eastward, they found a plain in Shinar and settled there. They said to each other, 'Come, let's make bricks and bake them thoroughly.' They used brick instead of stone, and tar instead of mortar. Then they said, 'Come, let us build ourselves a city, with a tower that reaches to the heavens, so that we may make a name for ourselves and not be scattered over the face of the whole earth.'

(Gn. 11:1–4)

When Cain had left home, he had sought refuge in an urban community. Just a few generations after the flood Noah's descendants were doing just the same. It is possible that this observation about men moving eastward has more than geographical significance. When Adam and Eve are expelled from the Garden of Eden it is in the eastward direction. When Cain is banished after the murder of Abel, he migrates to the land of wandering in the east. Here is just one more step in that same direction. It is as if the writer of Genesis wants to show us humanity moving progressively further and further away from paradise. The flood may have interrupted that movement for a moment, but it has not changed the direction. Man is still committed to his own alternative secularized Utopia, east of Eden. And Babel in many ways is the archetypal symbol of that Godless ambition.

Technological innovation

There is something in the aspiration of these migrants that, in spite of its ancient context, has a disturbingly contemporary ring. They have an enthusiasm for technological innovation. 'Let's make bricks and bake them thoroughly. Let's use brick instead of stone, tar instead of mortar.' A new environment proves to be an exciting intellectual challenge. As we said earlier, unlike animals, they do not need to wait for evolution to work at its long adaptations. They shape their own environment themselves. If there is no rock, they will bake mud bricks; if there is no mortar, they will use tar. And how childishly pleased they are with these improvements on previous engineering techniques. 'We can build towers now,' they say. 'Wow! What an idea!' New technology sparks off all kinds of thrilling new ideas. So scientific discovery becomes the prelude to cultural revolution and economic development. New cities, new architecture, new civilizations – we are familiar with such quantum leaps in human history. They have occurred many times, most recently in the industrial revolution of the eighteenth and nineteenth centuries. Many people believe that we are on the brink of just such a dramatic new advance today, as information technology transforms society yet again. There is nothing wrong with such progress, of course. Didn't God tell Adam to subdue the earth? Surely the architects of Babel were using their unique intellectual gifts to master their environment, just as God had mandated the human race to do. But what and why do people build? That is the question.

The forge that produces the plough can also shape the gun. The pen that writes poetry can also write pornography. The chisel that carves sculpture can also fashion idols. Almost certainly, this tower was a ziggurat designed to worship the stars. More than that, it was an obelisk to human pride. 'Let's make a city *for ourselves*,' they said. 'Let's make a name *for ourselves*.' This is mankind doing again what Adam did, pursuing its own path in defiance of God. 'Glory to man in the highest,' says the tower of Babel. 'He is the master of things.'

That devastating flood had not taught mankind much. Evil was mushrooming again. Pride, desire and arrogance were flourishing. Notice God's response to it this time: 'The LORD said, "If as one people speaking the same language they have begun to do this, then nothing they plan to do will be impossible for them"' (Gn. 11:6). The prospect of technological achievement which intoxicated the Babylonians disturbed God profoundly. He had a premonition of doom about it. 'Nothing they

69

plan to do will be impossible for them.' Can he mean that? Has he really invested such dreadful potential in us human beings? Well, he should know, for he created us.

Conservative-minded Christians often respond quite wrongly to the claims of humanism. They hear eminent scientists assuring us that one day soon we will visit the stars, create life from inorganic materials, build a computer with self-conscious identity, and so on. And they shake their heads and say, 'No, it's impossible. Only God can do such things. Proud man has grossly overestimated his abilities.' But that is not so. There is nothing inflated about the humanist's opinion of man's abilities. If he sets his mind unitedly and determinedly on a goal, man can achieve anything. God says so. 'Nothing . . . will be impossible for them.' But whereas that thought excites the humanist, it horrifies heaven. What on the lips of a humanist would be a glowing testimony of optimism about man's glorious future, becomes on the lips of God a grim foreboding of tragedy and disaster. For he knows what a dreadful responsibility omnipotence is. And he is utterly realistic about how irresponsible the human heart is. Humanity is simply not good enough to wield such power safely. That is why, ironically, the more our technology has grown, the more insecure we have become. God saw it all long ago. And he administered a remedy.

Utopian optimism is out

God said, '"Come, let us go down and confuse

their language so they will not understand each other." So the LORD scattered them from there all over the earth, and they stopped building the city' (Gn. 11:7–8). Many commentators treat this dispersion as if it were a judgment of God, but there is no indication of that in the text. We do not read that God was angry, simply that he was concerned about where man's foolish charge towards technological advance might lead him. Indeed, you could almost say that it was an act of mercy rather than retribution. Rather as a wise father will check his small son if he sees him running towards a fire, so God was diverting man's creative energies here from a suicidal course. Yet having said that, confusing human language was a very serious measure. More serious, perhaps, than we at first realize.

We are beginning to understand these days that languages are different not just superficially in their vocabulary but more fundamentally in the philosophy, logic and worldview they presuppose. Language does not simply express our thoughts, it shapes our thoughts. Its syntax controls the very way we comprehend things. So by diversifying human language God was introducing into the world a profound communication barrier, one which neither Esperanto nor bilingual interpreters would be able to amend. Human beings would no longer think the same way. Their aspirations, their values, their culture would diverge with the language. No longer would they all want the same kind of world. There would no longer be a consensus about truth. Nationalist rivalry would breed distrust, disagreement and competition.

It was all very regrettable. But it did mean that the technological revolution would progress more slowly. They stopped building the city. World empires would arise, of course, but they would now be short-lived, the nations would vie for supremacy and in the resulting collision cultural impetus would be lost. As in radiotherapy, harm would be done to good as well as to malignant tissue. Great achievements would be lost and never recovered. But in the wisdom of God it was better that way than to let the power of a fallen human race escalate unchecked. Better a world confused than a world which was single-mindedly going the wrong way.

There are profound lessons, then, in these early chapters of Genesis. Whatever field we are thinking about, we have to be realistic about the essential evilness of human beings. In our economics, as in our politics, Utopian optimism is out. We human beings will never build a paradise on earth – we will always spoil it.

A caution

We need to be wary of our technology too. We stand on the threshold of what Marshall McCluhan has called the electric era. New words are being invented, straining the English language to express the novelty of the new information age. The industrial revolution of the eighteenth and nineteenth centuries, they tell us, will be nothing compared with the transformation that is going to characterize post-industrial society. George Thompson, the Nobel Prize winner, suggests that not since the invention of agriculture at the commencement of the neolithic age has man stood on the brink of such momentous change. Perhaps it is significant that this potential revolution is all about the science of communication. The story of Babel instructs us to be suspicious of such aspirations. Technology gives power, and the more godlike that power is, the more dangerous it is for fallen man to wield it.

God's long-term plan

Maybe you find the story of Babel a rather unsatisfying one as far as our twentieth century is concerned. God's action here in confusing human languages seems very much to have been a stop-gap measure. It may have stopped them building the city then, but they are certainly building their skyscrapers again now, and with great success. What trick does God have up his sleeve this time, now that man's overweaning technology once again threatens to claim omnipotence? The answer to that, I am afraid, may seem laughably weak. It is there in Genesis 11, though I doubt you would recognize it: 'This is the account of Shem . . .' (Gn. 11:10). Your eye could slide over that phrase without a second look. Yet arguably, it is the most significant verse in the entire first eleven chapters of Genesis. Yes, Babel's confusion was a stop-gap, nothing more. God knew that sooner or later man's arrogance would reach crisis-point again. The diversification of language was just a pre-emptive strike to forestall that. To put it bluntly, God was playing for time. He had a plan, a plan of salvation. He had always had it. Unlike Noah's ark, this plan would rescue out of the jaws of his divine anger not just a single family but an innumerable multitude. It was a fantastic plan, so lofty in its conception that even the angels had no idea of it. It was a secret purpose hidden within the counsels of the Godhead from eternity past. But it was a long-term project. It needed time. And God intervened at the tower of Babel to give the world time. Time for what?

'This is the account of Shem. Two years after the flood, when Shem was 100 years old, he became the father of Arphaxad . . . When Arphaxad had lived 35 years, he became the father of Shelah . . . When Shelah had lived 30 years, he became the father of Eber . . .' (Gn. 11:10–14). It is rather a long list, so I won't bore you with it all. It is there so that we know why God needed time. For century after century the divided nations went their way. God did not interfere with them again – he didn't have to. He had checked the immediate danger. From now on his interest focused down on a single family among all those scattered peoples: a Semitic clan called Abraham. And it is there in the promise to Abraham that the Bible finds the ultimate answer to man's need of hope.

'Leave your country, your people and your father's household and go to the land I will show you,' said God (Gn. 12:1). Abraham began life in a city – a city of Babylonia, significantly. Archaeologists tell us it had a particularly fine ziggurat, but that is probably just coincidence. What is interesting is the direction in which Abraham's pilgrimage took him. God sent him west, not east.

At last man's drift away from paradise had been reversed. For Abraham was not looking for Babel. Babel was the city built by man. The New Testament tells us that Abraham was looking for a different city altogether – a better city with foundations, whose builder and maker was God.

Part three

Redemption

11

The Masterplan

It was Robbie Burns who made that famous comment about the best-laid schemes of mice and men. 'They gang oft agley,' he said – that is, 'They often go askew.' Whether you understand his dialect or not, you can't really fault his powers of observation. Human planning, even at its most thorough and precise, has a very poor track record.

Take the advertising campaign that was planned at huge expense by the manufacturers of Pepsi-Cola. They were trying for the first time to market their product in China, and they could not work out why sales kept falling rather than climbing as a result of all their hard work. Then somebody pointed out that their international slogan, 'Come alive with Pepsi', when translated into Mandarin, actually meant, 'Pepsi brings your ancestors back from the grave.' That's what they call a technical hitch! Many a well-laid plan has gone askew because of a problem like that.

Ferdinand Porsche, the builder of the Volkswagen motorcar, hit another technical hitch when he was ordered by Hitler in 1944 to design an invincible monster tank. It was to be 50 feet long with a larger calibre gun than any rival; it had to have armour plating so thick that it could withstand a direct hit by another tank; it had to be watertight, so it could be driven across rivers while totally submerged; and it had to be fast, powered by a 1500 horsepower engine. Porsche was delighted to prove his engineering expertise on the project. The only trouble was, when they built the prototype, it weighed 180 tons, with the result that every road it drove on was ruined, and when it tried to cross country it inevitably finished up buried up to its gunbarrel in mud. With uncharacteristic humour, the Germans code-named this vehicle 'the Mouse'. Well, Herr Porsche should have read his Robbie Burns before he started. The best-laid schemes of mice and men gang oft agley.

In the rest of this book we're going to be examining one scheme which is subject to no such technical hitches. It is an enterprise which, unlike Pepsi-Cola's advertising campaign, is victim to no blunders. It is a design which, unlike Herr Porsche's tank, totally meets its invincible specification. It is a scheme which, contrary to Burns' observation, can never go askew, precisely because it is a scheme laid down not by mice or by men but by God himself.

The plan of redemption

The Bible tells us that God formulated this great plan in the mists of eternity past. And for millennia it was a closely guarded secret, locked away in the deepest vault of his vast intelligence. But step by step the Masterplan has been put into action. Abraham's journey westward towards Canaan was a key stage in the plan. The Old Testament tells the story of many more stages: the captivity of Abraham's descendants in Egypt and the subsequent exodus; the giving of the law through Moses; the settlement in the Promised Land; the Davidic monarchy; the building of the temple; the exile in Babylon; the return to Jerusalem. But all this rich history was in fact leading up to one final denouement – the moment when the Masterplan would be finally accomplished and its secret unfolded.

One chapter of the New Testament that comes close to embracing the whole of the Masterplan is Romans 8. In Parts three and four of this book we are going to survey the teaching of this chapter of Scripture. Romans 8 is structured in three parts:

Verses 1–4	the past	– the part of God's plan that is already accomplished: a remedy for the guilt of sin.
Verses 5–17	the present	– the way we experience God's plan working out in our lives here and now.
Verses 18–39	the future	– what the plan holds out by way of hope for the days to come.

Before we begin, perhaps I should warn you that the going will not be easy. The cosmic purpose of God is the deepest mystery of the universe – it is far more demanding than general relativity or quantum electrodynamics!

My greatest satisfaction will be if you get excited and humbled and, yes, perhaps even dazzled by the profundity of Romans 8. Too many of us are content to paddle like infants in the shallows of the revelation of himself that God has given to us. It's a good thing to feel yourself stretched sometimes, to feel yourself out of your depth. Christianity would be boring if it didn't stretch us, if it didn't hold promise of inexhaustible riches yet to be explored. So I would prefer you to feel that it was all a little beyond you rather than that you smugly think, 'Boy, what a cinch this Christianity is!'

Romans 8 has challenged the best Christian minds throughout church history. Within its 39 verses it holds enough theology to keep hundreds of theologians busy for a lifetime. Yet it is also a passage of great pastoral value. I have decided that this is the chapter I want read to me when I am on my deathbed. For not only is God's eternal plan described more comprehensively and eloquently here than anywhere else in the whole of Scripture, but my personal place in that plan is also affirmed – yours too, if you are a Christian.

12

Our moral dilemma

Therefore, there is now no condemnation for those who are in Christ
Jesus, because through Christ Jesus
the law of the Spirit of life set me free
from the law of sin and death. For
what the law was powerless to do in
that it was weakened by the sinful
nature, God did by sending his own
Son in the likeness of sinful man to be
a sin offering. And so he condemned
sin in sinful man, in order that the
righteous requirements of the law
might be fully met in us, who do not
live according to the sinful nature but
according to the Spirit.

(Rom. 8:1–4)

First, we are going to look at the dimension of
God's Masterplan which is in the past tense: his
remedy for the guilt of sin. 'Therefore, there is
now no condemnation . . .' Notice that word '*now*'.
There has been a change. Once there was condemnation for sin, but there is *now* no condemnation
for those who are in Christ Jesus. Notice the use of

the past tense: 'God *did* by sending his own Son
. . . he *condemned* sin in sinful man.' This is something which has been accomplished by God in
Christ, and it has made a profound difference.

'God will forgive me. It's his business'

I am afraid a great many people underestimate
God's moral sensitivity. They assume it is easy for
God to forgive. After all, they say, the Bible tells us
that a forgiving spirit is a virtue. Surely, then, we
can depend on God's demonstration of such leni-
ency and tolerance himself. As the Empress Cath-
erine the Great is reputed to have said, 'Of course
God will forgive me. It's his business.' But it is by
no means as straightforward as that. And the
reason for that is tied up in the phrase you find in
Romans 8:4, 'the righteous requirements of the
law'.

It is upon God's righteousness that all moral
values in the universe depend. Take love, for
instance. Everybody agrees that love is bettter than
hate, but why? Our opinion on the matter cannot
possibly bind anybody but ourselves. The only
verdict which can turn love from being a human
preference into a moral imperative is the verdict of
God. It is because he is love that love is an absolute
by definition, irrespective of whether we agree or
not. In fact it is his will and character which define
all moral values. If God did not have a moral
character, there would be no morality in the universe except that which we invented for ourselves
for convenience. One consequence of this is that
God cannot treat sin lightly. If he were to overlook

a sin, no matter how minor, it would imply that right and wrong did not matter to him after all. We can overlook a sin with no such implication, for the righteousness of the universe does not hinge upon our moral consistency.

But God cannot overlook a sin like that. An accusation of moral indifference is one which he cannot allow to pass unchallenged. It is absolutely necessary for the preservation of moral order in his universe that his righteousness be undeniably demonstrated. And that means he must distance himself personally from every form of evil. He must take a clear stand against it. If he did not, the very meaning of the word 'righteousness' would be undermined.

Now, of course, the most obvious way in which God can achieve that moral distance from sin is by assuming the role of a judge, promulgating a law, defining the moral norms for which he stands and exacting penalties from those who break them. And that is indeed exactly what God has done. That is the meaning of the Ten Commandments. They are not arbitrary rules invented by God, much like an essay title thought up by a school-teacher. The Ten Commandments are a transcription into the imperative of God's own will and character. He says, 'You shall not murder' because he is the giver of all life. He says, 'You shall not give false testimony' because he is the source of all truth (Dt. 5:17, 20). God is intensely and personally committed to the 'righteous requirements of the law' of which Paul speaks in Romans 8:4. God cannot turn a blind eye to actions that fall short of those requirements. They are an offence against his person. We cannot break God's arm or God's leg. But we do injure and offend him by contradicting his moral character, and that is exactly what we do when we break his law.

Unfortunately, according to the apostle Paul, the Ten Commandments, for all their holiness and wisdom, are of little help to us human beings. For we just do not keep them. We cannot keep them even if we try to. As he puts it in Romans 8:3, 'the law was powerless' because 'it was weakened by the sinful nature'. Paul has spelled this out very personally in the previous chapter of the book of Romans. The law of God is holy and good, but for a fallen child of Adam such as he was, all attempts to keep that law could only end in misery and frustration. He says: 'I know that nothing good lives in me, that is, in my sinful nature. For I have the desire to do what is good, but I cannot carry it out' (Rom. 7:18). So the law becomes an instrument of condemnation. Indeed, he speaks of another 'law' which is at work in his personality, waging war against the moral aspirations of his mind and making him a prisoner to the power of sin (Rom. 7:23). This 'law', then, is not the law of God's righteous nature, but the law of Paul's own sinful nature.

The plight of human beings, as Paul analyses it in the book of Romans, is that God's law places us under its judgment. The Ten Commandments are very good at making us aware of what the righteous requirement of God is, but they are no use at all in enabling us to meet it. You may want to ask, 'Well, if that's so, why on earth did God bother to give us the Ten Commandments in the first place?

What's the use of a law like that?'

The answer is that God's law is given to us as a preparation for the gospel. Paul spells it out very clearly: 'we know,' he says, 'that whatever the law says, it says to those who are under the law, so that [here is the purpose of it] every mouth may be silenced and the whole world held accountable to God' (Rom. 3:19). No one will be declared righteous in God's sight by observing the law, because, as we have already said, our sinful nature prevents us from obeying it. But, says Paul, 'through the law we become conscious of sin' (Rom. 3:20).

There is a fine picture of this in *Pilgrim's Progress*. John Bunyan portrays a man with a book in his hand and a great burden on his back: 'As I looked, he read in the book and wept and trembled. "What shall I do to be saved?" he said.' And that is exactly Paul's point here. The Bible is not given to us initially to make us feel good. It is given to us initially to make us feel *bad*, to force us to acknowledge our moral incompetence, an incompetence which the Bible itself can do nothing to rectify. The Bible is given to us to confront us with the prospect of judgment, a judgment which the Bible, *per se*, can do nothing to avert.

Our greatest need

'Well,' you say again, 'pretty pointless, then, for God to give us the Bible. It borders on the sadistic. It's about as helpful as sending a condemned criminal a copy of the penal code. It's about as kind as sending the Hunchback of Notre-Dame a mirror for Christmas. "Dear Quasimodo, thought you'd like to see how hideous you are.'' What's the use of a Bible if all it can do is make us conscious of our guilt?' But in fact the Bible is a great deal of use. Diagnosis may not be a cure, but it is a necessary first step towards a cure. The X-ray may not take the cancer away, but it shows exactly where it is and what treatment it requires.

In the same way, Paul would say in another of his books, 'the law was our schoolmaster to bring us unto Christ' (Gal. 3:24, kjv). It is vital for God to expose our sin to us, because unless we feel it in all its horror and its intractability, unless we feel the helplessness of our bondage to our sinful nature, we will never, never desire to be free of it. This is the problem for very many of the people whom I try to talk to as a pastor.

What would the average person today identify, do you think, as his or her greatest need? Many newly-weds see their mortgage as their greatest burden. Many students see their final exams as their greatest anxiety. The middle-aged father's greatest problem is his teenage son. The unemployed person is desperate to find a job. The sick person is desperate to feel well again. There are dozens of felt needs which people have which seem the most vital issue in their lives. But they are all wrong. They are not seeing the human dilemma as God sees it. For our most fundamental need is an answer to our sin. This is where Christianity differs from most other great world religions, certainly from those Eastern religions that are sweeping in these days with the New Age movement. The fundamental problem of the human race is our moral failure, the way we have offended a righteous God. Our greatest need is for forgiveness. For we are guilty before God, and there is not a single thing that any of us can do about it.

Is there a way out? Can we be liberated from this crippling 'law of sin and death' (Rom. 8:2)? Can we escape this 'condemnation' to which it consigns us? The whole burden of Paul's good news is that '*now*' something has happened which means we can (Rom. 8:1–2).

13

'He died to make us good'

> For what the law was powerless to do
> in that it was weakened by the sinful
> nature, God did by sending his own
> Son in the likeness of sinful man to be
> a sin offering.
>
> (Rom. 8:3)

Paul is talking here about the most important thing
that has ever happened in the history of the world.
He is explaining to us why Jesus had to die on the
cross. Now we all know about the cross, don't we?
Christians talk about it in what sometimes seems
to be a rather gory fashion. We make much of the
blood of Christ. And if we have had any Sunday
School training at all, we know that according to
the Christian message, the blood of Christ has
something to do with forgiveness. As the children's hymn says: 'He died that we might be
forgiven, he died to make us good, that we might
go at last to heaven, saved by his precious blood.'
But though many people have some vague notion
of this kind, I find that the vast majority of people,
even Christian people these days, have practically
no understanding at all of precisely *how* Christ's

death on a cross 2,000 years ago is connected with their experience of being forgiven by God today.

Why the cross?

Many people try to interpret the cross, I find, as if it were a kind of influence upon us. We look at the cross and we feel conscience-stricken about our sin. We determine to put our lives in order. So Christ's death becomes a kind of model of love that moves us to be better people. Now, of course, there is an element of truth in that. The cross is a powerful emotional symbol. Many people have been intensely moved and changed by its dramatic power.

But that kind of view of the cross, which sees it only as an influence on us, is really open to insuperable objections. For a start, if you think about it, it savours of a particularly pernicious form of moral blackmail. Do we really believe that God, faced by a morally rebellious world, would try to manipulate us with emotional levers? It puts the cross in the same category as an IRA hunger strike: a gesture which achieves nothing except to embarrass those who have to watch it. But more than that, this interpretation of the cross is fundamentally irrational.

Just think for a moment. Imagine a boy and a girl having an argument. The girl says the boy doesn't love her. The boy insists he does love her. 'All right,' he says, 'to resolve our argument, if you really want me to prove that I love you, I will go and throw myself off a cliff.' Does that make any sense to you? It doesn't make any sense to me, because I can't see any connection between him throwing himself off a cliff and love. For a death to prove love, the loved one must benefit in some way from the death. If the girl were drowning, say, and the fellow dashes in at the risk of his life to save her, and perishes in the attempt, I can see that might show how much he loved her. But there's no love in giving your life up for nothing. Similarly, the trouble with these theories which see the cross as merely an influence or example is that Christ's death does not benefit us directly in any way. They reduce the cross to a meaningless gesture. Indeed, you could argue that he would have had much more influence and been a much better example if he had stayed alive. To put it another way, the problem with these views is that they are totally subjective. They suggest that the purpose of the cross is to affect our *attitude* to our sin. That is not right. Whatever grain of truth there may be in that point of view, what Paul is saying here in Romans 8 is quite the opposite. He is saying that the cross makes a difference, not to how *we feel* about our sins, but to how *God feels* about our sins.

Think of some situation in which you have been sinned against, profoundly damaged by somebody else's selfishness in some way. Perhaps you have fallen in love and got engaged or maybe even married. Then you have found that the person who you thought was promised to you has been unfaithful to you. Or maybe you have been the victim of child abuse, or racial discrimination, or criminal assault. Maybe you have lost a loved one at the hands of a drunken driver, or even a terrorist bomb. Whenever someone sins against us it hurts profoundly; it hurts to feel rejected; it hurts to suffer loss. And you have to do something with that hurt. You can't pretend it isn't there. Of course, one way of dealing with it is to get angry. Angry with that unfaithful partner; angry with that negligent parent; with that racist, with that mugger, with that drunkard, with that terrorist. There is nothing wrong with anger. It is a perfectly legitimate righteous indignation which we feel. Everybody feels it when their human rights are trampled upon. Yet anger is a destructive passion. Anger tears relationships apart. It leaves us feeling isolated and bitter. It may preserve our pride, but it is more like amputating the wounded limb than truly healing the injury.

The way of love

Fortunately, anger is not the only way to deal with hurt. There is another way. The way of love. This way isn't easy. It isn't cheap. For that hurt still has to be handled. But the extraordinary thing about love is that it has the power not to ignore hurt but to absorb hurt; to take it into itself and to consume it and to digest it; to come to terms with injury in such a way that instead of a relationship being blown apart by it, there is the possibility of for-giveness, of reconciliation, of a new beginning. And that is the way God chose on the cross: the way of love.

He is angry with our sins; he feels that anger, but there in Jesus' suffering, we see him absorbing the pain, absorbing the wrath. The Bible assures

93

us, 'God was reconciling the world to himself in Christ,' and it invites us to be so reconciled to God: 'God made him who had no sin to be sin for us, so that in him we might become the righteousness of God' (2 Cor. 5:19, 21). That is exactly what Paul is trying to get across to us here. The law could not do it, but God did it nevertheless 'by sending his own Son in the likeness of sinful man to be a sin offering' (Rom. 8:3).

Every Jew knew that before you could be forgiven by God an animal had to die. Its blood had to be shed. That blood symbolized the seriousness of sin in God's eyes. It was shed to satisfy his holiness, to avert his anger from the worshipper. In the same way, says Paul, Christ was our sin offering. No one can say to God, when he forgives you and me, 'God, you're being morally indifferent. You're letting this criminal go free. You don't care about sin.' God replies, 'You say I don't care about sin? But look at the cross!' He points to Jesus' broken body and shed blood and he says, 'There – that's how much I care about sin. It's true that I've left their sins unpunished, but this mercy I exercise towards them doesn't impugn my righteousness, for I have demonstrated that righteousness. To the shock of the universe I have come down and borne the punishment they deserved. I have condemned their sin already in my Son.'

The cross, then, is not an attempt at moral blackmail; neither is it an irrational gesture. The cross is the place where God made forgiveness possible. The cross enables him to be 'just and yet the justifier' of people who believe in Jesus. Because of the cross, and only because of the cross, you and I can go free. 'There is now no condemnation,' sums up Paul, 'for those who are in Christ Jesus' (Rom. 8:1). By means of this sacrifice a new principle has been unleashed in the universe; not the principle of moral weakness, which is at work in us human beings, and which renders righteousness impossible for us and condemnation inevitable; not the law of sin and death. No, this new principle Paul calls 'the law of the Spirit of life', because it has the power to emancipate us from our former wretchedness. By means of this new principle which Jesus has introduced, the seemingly impossible has been accomplished. The righteous requirement of the law is fully met in us. We are acquitted; we are 'justified', to use Paul's word. It is just as if we had never sinned.

Get hold of this!

Inevitably, among the readers of this book there are going to be some who are still labouring in their Christian lives with a feeling of personal unworthiness. Perhaps you hear people giving marvellous testimonies and inspiring addresses, and you hear people saying frightfully holy things, but inside you're just withering away. You're thinking, 'This just isn't where I'm at. Oh, I can put on a good mask. I can make people believe I'm just as "Christian" as they are. But when I get on my own with God, I just crumple, because I know how much failure there is in me. I feel so tormented by that besetting sin that keeps haunting me. And because of it the devil keeps telling me,

"It's no good you thinking you can ever do anything for God in your life. You're a hypocrite!"'

Do you see what the answer to that is? It's right there in Romans 8. God has remedied the guilt of sin. The Masterplan has swung into action, and today you and I are the beneficiaries of it. All we have to do is hold out the empty hands of faith to receive the freedom from condemnation which Christ has obtained for us. 'There is now no condemnation for those who are in Christ Jesus.' Get hold of that!

14

A faith that works

God's plan has already remedied the guilt of sin. It has happened already, past tense. But Paul goes on very quickly in Romans 8 to fill us in on phase 2 of this plan, closely connected to phase 1. He says that phase 2 counteracts the *power* of sin, here and now, *present tense*. Look at Romans 8:5–9:

> Those who live [present tense] according to the sinful nature have their minds set on what that nature desires; but those who live in accordance with the Spirit have their minds set on what the Spirit desires. The mind of sinful man is death, but the mind controlled by the Spirit is life and peace, because the sinful mind is hostile to God. It does not submit to God's law, nor can it do so. Those controlled by the sinful nature cannot please God. You, however, are controlled not by the sinful nature but by the Spirit.

The trouble with the word 'free' that Paul used

in verse 2 is that it is so easily misunderstood. Indeed, one of Paul's greatest fears in writing this letter to the Romans is that people *will* misunderstand it. He knew from experience how easy it is to turn liberty into licence. And it is not difficult to see how that could happen in the context of what he has just been saying about the achievement of Jesus' death on the cross. '"There is now no condemnation for those who are in Christ Jesus." Wow! You mean that we Christians can do whatever we like and get away with it? What an opportunity!'

But that would be an erroneous deduction, and in these verses Paul explains why. In fact he hardly draws a breath before he addresses the issue. Look again at verse 4: '. . . in order that the righteous requirements of the law might be fully met in us, who do not live according to the sinful nature but according to the Spirit.' There are some writers who think that when Paul talks about 'the righteous requirements of the law' being 'fully met in us', he means that God enables Christians to overcome their sins so that they actually become righteous on their own account. But there can be no doubt, I think, that Paul's meaning is not that at all. It would contradict everything he has argued for in the earlier chapters of Romans if he were arguing here that Christ saves us by enabling us to save ourselves. No, the righteous requirements of the law are fully met in us not because we have found some spiritual secret of moral perfection, but because our sin has already been condemned through the offering of Christ on the cross on our behalf.

Belief and behaviour

Having said that, however, it is important to notice how closely Paul links that doctrine of justification (as it is often called) with the issue of our *present tense* Christian conduct. Suppose we were to ask Paul, 'How do you tell who the people are who are "in Christ" and who as a result do not come into condemnation? How do you know who those people are in whom the righteous requirements of the law have been fully met, so that God's righteousness is satisfied?'

Paul's answer would not be a confessional one. It would be a behavioural one. He says it is those who do not live according to the sinful nature who are so justified. This is of enormous importance. It means that the work of Christ Jesus is not just to acquit us judicially. His work also functions to empower us morally. It does not just free us from the judgment of God; it frees us from the moral bondage to sin that placed us under judgment in the first place. And what you and I have got to get hold of is that these two liberations always go together. They are welded together inseparably. You cannot experience the one without experiencing the other. As Paul puts it in verse 9, 'You . . . are controlled not by the sinful nature but by the Spirit, if the Spirit of God lives in you. And if anyone does not have the Spirit of Christ, he does not belong to Christ.' There is no possibility, then, that a person can enjoy the saving work of Christ delivering them from the condemnation of sin, without also demonstrating the saving work of Christ delivering them from the power of sin; the two things go together, both mediated by the Spirit of Christ. And if you don't have that Spirit in you, releasing you from the grip of the sinful nature, then, Paul says, your claim to be a Christian is ill founded.

The Spirit of Easter

We tend to associate the Holy Spirit with the Day of Pentecost. However, in Romans 8:10–11 Paul associates the Spirit much more closely with Easter:

> If Christ is in you, your body is dead because of sin, yet your spirit is alive because of righteousness. And if the Spirit of him who raised Jesus from the dead is living in you, he who raised Christ from the dead will also give life to your mortal bodies through his Spirit, who lives in you.

Paul is explaining here why Jesus not only had to die, but also had to rise. When he rose from the dead Christ became available to his disciples in a new way. He who was once with them as a friend was now able to dwell in them as a spirit, the Holy Spirit, who is none other than the Spirit of the risen Jesus. Notice that Paul draws no distinction in these verses between talking about 'Christ' being in you, the 'Spirit' being in you, or the 'Spirit of Christ' being in you. These are all ways of describing the same truth, namely that as a result of his resurrection Jesus is able to dwell in his disciples and renew them spiritually and morally. One day, Paul says, that renewal will be complete. Our very physical bodies will be given new life by the Spirit, just as Jesus was raised from the dead that first Easter morning. But that is a brief glimpse into the future. Right at this moment in time the Spirit of Christ is concentrating his renewing work on the inside of our personalities. He is leaving our bodies for the moment in their natural state of mortality and weakness. But he has regenerated our minds, that inner part of our personality which is the centre of our human will and understanding. He has made our minds new. So Paul says in verse 6: 'The mind of sinful man is death, but the mind controlled by the Spirit is life and peace.'

Radio-controlled Christians?

I must say, I am a bit irritated by the way the NIV uses the word 'controlled' in its translation here. There is really no word in the Greek text that means 'controlled', and the NIV's use of this word can encourage people in some rather odd ideas. Some people seem to think that being 'controlled' by the Spirit means being subject to a continuous stream of strange inner promptings. They won't do anything till 'the Spirit tells them to do it'. I once met a student who would not get up in the morning till the Spirit so directed him. It was about the most imaginative excuse for missing lectures I ever heard! Now Paul is not talking about any such thing. This idea of a radio-controlled Christian, whose every action is supernaturally directed by signals received from on high, is hopelessly mistaken.

The Spirit of God does not *replace* our mind. He *renews* our mind. It is no part of God's intention to rob us of our self-determination. What he wants is not a Spirit-controlled robot, but a Spirit-informed man or woman – a new man, a new woman, with a mind which is willing and able to offer intelligent obedience to his law. Formerly, we could not do this, for the sinful mind was hostile to God. It did not submit to God's law, nor could it do so. In our former state, Paul says, pleasing God was something we just could not do.

Now that the Masterplan has been put into action, now that Jesus has come, died and risen again, all that has been changed. Not only has he granted us freedom from the judgment, but he has granted us freedom from moral bondage as well. 'Therefore, brothers,' says Paul, 'we have an obligation – but it is not to the sinful nature, to live according to it.' No, we have to live according to the Spirit. 'If you live according to the sinful nature, you will die; but if by the Spirit you put to death the misdeeds of the body, you will live' – you identify yourself as one of those who are alive to God. 'Those who are led by the Spirit of God are sons of God' (Rom. 8:12–14).

This, of course, has very important implications for us. It means there can be absolutely no moral complacency in a Christian's life. It means we cannot even begin to allow ourselves that thought. 'No condemnation? Then I can do what I like and get away with it?' Absolutely not. Notice here that Paul does not say, 'If you live according to the sinful nature you will be a backslider.' He does not say, 'If you live according to the sinful nature you are a carnal Christian and will get an inferior seat in the heavenly glory.' He says, 'If you live according to the sinful nature you will die.' He refuses, in other words, to give assurance of salvation to Christians whose lives are not giving evidence of moral change. Paul shows us that forgiveness and renewal belong together. You cannot separate them.

15

New relationship, new destiny

In days gone by, theologians used to talk about a great doctrine of the Bible known as 'the perseverance of the saints'. It tells us that if you are a true child of God you can never be lost, because God is committed to you. Once you are in Christ, God never will take you out of Christ again. That is a great doctrine and, I believe, a very true one. But we must never pervert that doctrine of the perseverance of the saints and turn it into a doctrine of the perseverance of sinners. If we are real Christians we will be different. We have to be different. For we do not live according to our sinful nature. We live according to the Spirit. If we are not living that way, then, says Paul, by our conduct we deny the identity which we profess. Paul is adamant, then. We are no longer under the power of sin as we used to be, and it will show.

Where's the family likeness?

Let me say to you very frankly, then, that if you are giving in to sin right now, if there are things in your life which you know are offensive to God, and you are just tolerating them – if you are not fighting them, you are not wrestling with God about them, if you are not trying as hard as you know how to claim this moral power of the Holy Spirit to overcome those things – then it is no wonder that your spiritual life is dry, and that you lack assurance that you are a Christian. A person who lives like that has no right to assurance. God assures only those who are demonstrating, by the distinctiveness of their lifestyle, that the Spirit of Christ is within them.

You claim to be a child of God. Where is the family likeness? That is the question. This great plan of God unites these two prongs. It remedies our guilt but it also counteracts the power of sin. God assures only those who have by virtue of Christ's death passed from condemnation into life if they are simultaneously demonstrating through their lifestyle that they are waging war against the misdeeds of the body, by the Spirit's power. You may say to yourself, 'I'm aware that there are areas in my life where I'm failing. How do I claim this power of the Spirit to live a better life, a life where the power of sin has less control over me?' Notice once again Paul's emphasis on that word 'mind'. In Romans 8:5 he says: 'Those who live in accordance with the Spirit have their minds set on what the Spirit desires.' The clue to the breaking of the power of sin in our lives is the *mind*; in particular, where we 'set' our mind.

In Greek mythology there was a certain island inhabited by the sirens. Half woman and half bird, they spent their days beguiling passing sailors with their entrancing songs and luring them to shipwreck on the rocks. When he had to pass by the island of the sirens, the hero Odysseus stopped his ears with wax and tied himself to the mast of his ship so that he could not be seduced by them. On the other hand, when the Argonauts passed by the island, Orpheus used a different strategy. He took a harp and played music of such superior charm that the sailors gave no heed to the sirens. That is the way Jesus seeks to destroy the love of sin in us: not by stern external threats such as the law administered, not by the threat of judgment. There is no more possibility of condemnation for those who belong to him. He does not want us to feel tyrannized by that threat. Now his tactic is to place within us a new longing for holiness. The Spirit charms us, placing within our minds a new focus for our attention. Like Orpheus, he woos our hearts from those evil things that seek to enchant us, and he leads us to a higher and better aspiration.

What is your dream?

If you want to know how to conquer the power of sin in your life, the answer is to fill your mind with better things, noble things, good things, holy things. Stop surrendering your mind to those things that you know drag you down. That does not mean that you have to be perfect. The apostle Paul candidly admitted in this letter to the Romans that he continued to be frustrated by his sinful nature, Christian though he was. He was still only partially renewed. He still had that fallen sinful nature. He could not shed it till death. Until then, he was a man of two worlds. He belonged to the race of Adam and he belonged to the race of Christ simultaneously, and in consequence he found himself torn. He speaks of the flesh warring with the Spirit within him. That is a conflict which all Christians know. So I am not asking, 'Are you perfect?' We will never be able to claim that. But I am asking, 'Do you want to be perfect? Is that your dream?' John Newton said, 'I'm not what I ought to be, I'm not what I want to be, I'm not what I hope to be, but by the grace of God I'm not what I once was.' That is a Christian testimony for the here and now. If that is true of you, two other things are also going to be true of you.

The first is that you have a new relationship with God. 'Those who are led by the Spirit of God are sons of God,' says Paul. 'You did not receive a spirit that makes you a slave again to fear, but you received the Spirit of sonship. And by him we cry, "*Abba*, Father." The Spirit himself testifies with our spirit that we are God's children' (Rom. 8:14–16). One of the most profound truths that Jesus reveals to us is that fatherhood is something absolutely fundamental to the Godhead. Always, in eternity, in the heart of God, there was a Son. And yet even more overwhelming and extraordinary is the claim that Paul makes here – that God intends to take us human beings and place us in that same position of filial privilege and intimacy which Jesus has. We too are to be his children, children by adoption, brothers and sisters of Christ. Think about that! That is why we can pray '*Abba*, Father, Daddy' with such intimacy, such candour, such affection. A new relationship with God will be yours if you are one of those in whom the power of sin is being broken by the inner working of the Holy Spirit.

But not only that. In addition to a new relationship with God, you will also have a new destiny. 'If we are children, then we are heirs – heirs of God and co-heirs with Christ, if indeed we share in his sufferings in order that we may also share in his glory' (Rom. 8:17). God's plan has not reached its culmination yet. He has already done marvellous things. In the past, through the cross, he has remedied the guilt of sin. Here and now, by the Spirit, he is counteracting the power of sin. But his plan will not have reached its culmination till one day in the future he eliminates every consequence of sin and restores to us that paradise which he has always wanted to share with us and which Paul here calls 'glory'.

Part four

New creation

16

Living in hope

Eeyores and Micawbers

Are you an optimist or a pessimist? You know the difference, of course. The optimist believes that we live in the best of all possible worlds, and the pessimist fears that this is so. Most people fall into one of these two camps. They are either confident Micawbers who always look on the bright side of things or morbid Eeyores who invariably expect the worst. And not infrequently, Christians bring their natural temperament in this regard into their theology. Christian optimists are technically called post-millennialists by those who like long words. Post-millennialists are hugely confident of the power of the gospel to transform the world. They talk triumphalistically of how they are going to claim territory for Christ, bind Satan by their prayers, bring in the kingdom of God by their miracles. They are great optimists.

Christian pessimists, on the other hand, are called pre-millennialists by those who like long words. They are much less sanguine. They point to those texts which speak about evil men waxing worse and worse, about tares sown among the wheat; they emphasize Jesus' statement that the way to eternal life is narrow and only a few will find it. 'No,' they say, 'the church of Jesus Christ must always be a persecuted minority. There is no way we can expect to transform the world. The manifestation of the kingdom of God must wait until Jesus comes again.'

Who is right, do you think? The optimist or the pessimist? Well, I want to suggest that, as is so often the case in Christian controversy, they are both right and they are both wrong. The danger of the Christian optimist is that he may expect too much. The danger of the Christian pessimist is that he may expect too little. We need to have a balanced perspective on this issue, and Romans 8 is the ideal chapter to help us in this.

As we have seen, some of God's plan has already been implemented by the death of Jesus on the cross. He has already remedied the guilt of sin, past tense. 'There is now no condemnation for those who are in Christ Jesus' (Rom. 8:1). And by the Spirit of the risen Jesus, God is now (present tense) counteracting the power of sin in our lives. Christ is in you, Paul is saying. You are not under obligation any longer to serve your sinful nature. Put together, those two things constitute the '*now*' of Christian experience. These are the things we may legitimately expect to enter into. These are the things the Bible encourages us to claim by faith, depending on the promises of God, and they are great and far-reaching realities. But it is important not to overstate them or to go beyond them. The fact is, the consequences of sin are still very much with us.

We still live in a fallen world. We are still tied to

mortal bodies, bodies of death. We still have a morally corrupt nature within us, even though it is counteracted by the Spirit of Jesus. And it is vital that we are realistic about the limitations which these things place upon us. They impose an inevitable frustration upon us. We Christians cannot be Utopians. Triumphalistic optimism about what we can achieve in the world, even when we have the Holy Spirit of the risen Jesus within us, is out of place and invites disillusionment. What the Bible offers us in regard to these tragic consequences of sin in us and in our world is not immediate deliverance. What the Bible offers us as far as these things are concerned is a future hope. You see, the plan is not complete. There is a third and unfulfilled phase. The same God who remedied the guilt of sin by Jesus' death, the same God who is counteracting the power of sin by Jesus' Spirit, will one day eliminate the consequences of sin by Jesus' return. And that constitutes the 'not yet' of Christian experience: the things we do not have now but which we are waiting for. Waiting, I hasten to add, not wistfully or uncertainly. No, this plan, unlike the plans of mice and men, will not 'gang agley'. The might and the majesty of an omnipotent, sovereign God are energizing it. This plan is going to happen!

So let us look at the final section of Romans 8 with that in mind. God has a plan to eliminate the consequences of sin one day. It is a plan that cannot fail.

The hope of glory

Paul begins to spell it all out in verses 17–18: 'if . . . we share in his sufferings . . . we may also share in his glory. I consider that our present sufferings are not worth comparing with the glory that will be revealed in us.' It makes all the difference to have something to look forward to. Just think how the dull, cold and depressing British winter is made more tolerable by a few holiday brochures. The expectation of those sun-drenched beaches that we will be sprawled upon in July makes the awful winter weather seem less of a burden somehow. Well, says Paul, when it comes to that kind of anticipation, the Bible has something even better to offer than the Costa Brava. The Christian is looking forward to a stupendous prospect that makes the very worst that can possibly happen on this planet seem trivial and inconsequential.

'Our present sufferings are not worth comparing with the glory,' says Paul. Yes, that is the word he uses. One day we are going to inherit 'glory'. What does he mean by that word, do you think? I will tell you what he does not mean. He does not mean wafting around upon a cloud, clothed in a celestial négligé, strumming a golden harp. Our Christian hope is not that we will 'go to heaven'. Rather, Paul speaks in Romans 8 of the inheritance of a new creation. Think about that. A new creation. Nothing less. Peter says the same: 'in keeping with his promise we are looking forward to a new heaven and a new earth, the home of righteousness' (2 Pet. 3:13). What was it Jesus said the meek will inherit? The second cloud on the right past

Mars? 'The meek . . . will inherit the earth,' he said (Mt. 5:5). Glory in Paul's mind is not some imponderable vapour. It is solid. It is substantial. It is a new heaven and a new earth.

The trouble with many of us is that we have taken the hints which the Bible gives about the intermediate state in which a Christian survives death, and we have turned that nebulous existence into a kind of permanent and eternal expectation, as if existence as some kind of disembodied spirit were the best God had in mind for us. It is not so. Christians do not confess the immortality of the soul. That is a pagan doctrine, Christians believe in the resurrection of the body. Do you see the difference? We are waiting for a new heaven and a new earth. But many Christians have gone astray on that.

That is why George Bernard Shaw claimed, in his usual pugnacious way, that heaven as conventionally conceived was a place so inane, so dull, so useless, so miserable, that nobody would ever venture to describe a whole day in heaven, though plenty of people have described a day at the seaside. Shaw had listened to too many Christians who were not waiting for a new heaven and a new earth. Shaw was a socialist, passionately concerned for justice, for human fulfilment, for human dignity. A strumming harp on cloud nine had no appeal for him. Perhaps if someone had told him that Christians were waiting for a new earth in which righteousness dwells, he might have been less of a sceptic. We Christians do not have to be browbeaten by those who call our future hope an opiate for the people. We are looking for a just society too. We believe in such a world. We are waiting for such a world. The prospect of such a world is what motivates us. It is that coming kingdom which we celebrate. The difference is that when the inveterate forces of evil frustrate our best endeavours, when the revolution turns sour, when our man-made Utopian ventures fail, then the Christian does not collapse in despair. We do not give up on the future. We know there is a 'not yet' in our experience. It has to be there. For we cannot create this new world order ourselves. The New Jerusalem must come down out of heaven.

Glory in the here and now

'I do not think in the last forty years I have lived one conscious hour that was not influenced by the thought of our Lord's return.' Who do you think said that? You may be amazed to learn that it was Anthony Ashley Cooper, better known as Lord Shaftesbury. This man probably did more to improve the welfare of the poor and disadvantaged in the nineteenth century than any other single individual. He reformed the treatment of the insane, he pioneered legislation against the exploitation of labour in factories, he sponsored low-cost urban housing, and free education for destitute children. One biographer, who is far from uncritical of certain aspects of his life, says no one has ever done more to lessen the extent of human misery and to add to the sum total of human happiness.

If a man like Shaftesbury were active today, we would almost certainly assume that he was a left-wing militant. But he was not. He was a Christian.

He was the leader of the evangelical wing of the Church of England and the President of the British and Foreign Bible Society. Christians are sometimes accused of being too heavenly minded to be any earthly use, aren't they? Shaftesbury's testimony proves just how spurious and misguided that analysis is. Far from anaesthetizing his social conscience, Shaftesbury's biblicism was a constant spur to his reforming zeal. And what aspect of his biblicism? 'I do not think in the last forty years I have lived one conscious hour that was not influenced by the thought of our Lord's return.' That is Christianity. Unlike the spurious hope of Marxism, our hope does not make us ashamed. Our hope does not lead us into false Utopian dreams that will come crashing down round our head. We are going to inherit glory, the resurrection glory of Christ, a glory that will surround us with a wonderful new world. But more than that, the glory of Christ will transform us at last into the new people we really want to be. Do you notice that Paul says in Romans 8:17 that we will not merely see God's glory, but we will 'share' it? This glory, he says, will not just be revealed 'to us', it will be revealed '*in us*' (v. 18).

Too heavenly minded to be any earthly use? Paul's emphasis here is rather that unless we are a little bit heavenly minded we cannot be Christians at all. For to be a Christian is by definition to be oriented towards the future. It is to live with the taste of glory in your mouth. But having said that, notice how carefully Paul balances the intoxicating prospect of this 'not yet' with blunt realism about the 'now'.

17

Facing the fact of suffering

We share in Christ's sufferings, Paul says, 'in order that we may also share in his glory. I consider that our present sufferings are not worth comparing with the glory that will be revealed in us' (Rom. 8:17–18). That word 'suffering' is important. Paul clearly believed that the present, the 'now', was characterized by suffering. We must experience that suffering, he says, just as Jesus himself did. Indeed, our willingness to participate in his Good Friday agony is a necessary condition of our participation in the radiance of his Easter joy. We share his sufferings in order that we may share his glory. It is no part of Christian religion, then, to shut our eyes to suffering and pretend it isn't there. We live in a fallen and broken world, a world which is no longer as God intended it to be. So sickness and hardship and calamity and oppression and war and death – these things inevitably afflict us. We do not romanticize about them; we do not disguise them with verbal cosmetics. We name them for what they are: evils. And the fact that we are Christians does not render us immune to these evils any more than Christ himself was immune to them. On the contrary. It is our task, says Paul, to accept suffering as he did, as the inevitable consequence of our identification with this present evil age.

Where Christians are different is that they have something to look forward to, a time when that suffering will be no more. And they are not looking forward to it alone:

> The creation waits in eager expectation for the sons of God to be revealed. For the creation was subjected to frustration, not by its own choice, but by the will of the one who subjected it, in hope that the creation itself will be liberated from its bondage to decay and brought into the glorious freedom of the children of God.
>
> (Rom. 8:19–21)

Whose fault?

Fascinating words, these! We might wish that Paul had developed his thoughts a little more fully, for without doubt, behind these verses lie all those insights from Genesis that we looked at earlier in this book. This world was made with human beings as its intended viceroys; human beings, made in the image of God, were to have dominion over God's world. They were to be the stewards of his universe. And when mankind, the pinnacle of creation, fell into sin, the natural world also fell victim to a curse. It isn't Mother Nature's fault, says Paul, that there is so much suffering around; it's our fault. We human beings are ultimately to blame. We have abdicated our proper role as stewards of God's universe, and, as a result, the whole of creation is out of gear. There is a spanner in the works. The universe is 'subjected to frustration' and is in 'bondage to decay'.

Perhaps a picture devised by the scholar C. E. B. Cranfield will help. Think of a great orchestra assembled in the Royal Albert Hall to play Handel's *Messiah*. The instrumentalists are all there, poised to contribute their distinctive note or harmony. The choir is there, ready to burst forth in chorus. But this whole magnificent scene is frozen. It is in a state of suspended animation. Indeed, it has been frozen into immobility for so long now that dust is covering the violins and cobwebs have grown over the soprano's gown. What's wrong? Somebody is missing. The performance can't begin till the conductor takes the rostrum.

But this conductor is of such a perverse temperament that he has decided that he would rather write his own music than beat time to somebody else's. So he has abandoned the stage and can be found instead privately humming tuneless self-compositions in his dressing-room while practising grandiose sweeps of his baton in front of the mirror.

In the same way, says Paul, the whole magnificent orchestra of the universe, with all the splendid chorus of sub-human life, has been rendered pointless because the one who ought to be the leader of its hymn to God's praise has deserted his post. Namely, us, mankind. And not until men and women have been restored to their unique position as sons and daughters of God, bearing the image of their Maker and ruling the world as his deputies, can the universe rediscover its true meaning. Until that restoration is accomplished, Mother Nature must suffer as if 'in the pains of childbirth' (Rom. 8:22), longing, says Paul, for the liberation which only the manifestation of the children of God can provide. Why, says Paul, if only we had ears tuned into the fundamental frequencies involved, we would realize that the whole universe has been sighing with impatience for millennia in anticipation of that glorious freedom to come. Indeed, that is precisely the point. To be a Christian is to vibrate in sympathy with those cosmic groans: 'we ourselves, who have the firstfruits of the Spirit, groan inwardly as we wait eagerly for our adoption as sons, the redemption of our bodies' (Rom. 8:23).

Not yet

Now Paul made it clear in Romans 8:15 that Christians are rightly called the sons and daughters of God here and now, because the Spirit of sonship or adoption dwells in them, leading them to lift their hearts to God and say, 'Father'. But even though the sonship of Christian believers is a present-tense reality, part of the 'now', we have to face the fact that it is nevertheless an incognito identity. Apart from that partial and imperfect moral renewal which the Holy Spirit is working in our lives, there is no glaringly obvious and unambiguous evidence of our sonship. Even its sacramental sign, baptism, leaves no external mark upon us. Our physical bodies are indistinguishable from anybody else's. That is why we are still vulnerable to suffering. That is why Paul cries out at the end of Romans 7, tormented with frustration at the fallenness of his human nature, 'What a wretched man I am! Who will rescue me from this body of death?' (v. 24).

Indeed, even our so-called spiritual life is rendered imperfect, hindered by the same human inadequacies. Thus Paul writes in Romans 8:26: 'In the same way, the Spirit helps us in our weakness. We do not know what we ought to pray.' The folly of our human ignorance and the bitterness of our human suffering and the inveteracy of our human sinfulness all so easily conspire to spoil the intimacy of our filial relationship with God. Often we could not communicate with God at all if it were not for the special ministry of the Holy Spirit in our lives. For, says Paul, when we are reduced to a state of prayerlessness by our human weakness, the Spirit nevertheless goes on praying for us, identifying us as the children of God even when we have temporarily lost the assurance of our divine pedigree. 'We do not know what we ought to pray, but the Spirit himself intercedes for us with groans that words cannot express. And he who searches our hearts knows the mind of the Spirit, because the Spirit intercedes for the saints in accordance with God's will' (Rom. 8:26–27). What a lot of groaning is going on, then! The universe is groaning, the Christians are groaning, even the Holy Spirit is groaning, joining his wordless sighs to ours, begging God to accomplish his will, to complete the Masterplan.

But at the moment, says Paul, that is all that

even the Holy Spirit can do for us. True, he is a marvellous sample of heaven. As Paul puts it in verse 23, the Spirit is 'the firstfruits', a foretaste of that glory to come. But it would be a mistake to exaggerate the degree to which even the Holy Spirit can offset the effects of our fallenness this side of Christ's return. For the fact is that our resurrection still lies in the future. The resurrection is part of the 'not yet'. As Paul says in verse 23, 'we wait eagerly for . . . the redemption of our bodies', and in that sense our adoption as sons is incomplete. We are not yet restored as triumphant monarchs over God's world, though sometimes in the songs we sing we like to pretend that we are. No, the universe is still out of joint. We are still victims of its brokenness; we still get ill; we can still be hurt; we still sin; we still die, and so do our loved ones.

As things stand, despite the glorious ministry of the Holy Spirit within us, we Christians have to believe in our divine sonship against all kinds of emotionally compelling evidence to the contrary. Paul says that it is precisely that act of believing in our heavenly destiny, even though as yet it is unseen and unseeable, which identifies us as Christians: 'In this hope we were saved. But hope that is seen is no hope at all. Who hopes for what he already has? But if we hope for what we do not yet have, we wait for it patiently' (Rom. 8:24–25).

To adapt some lines of Oscar Wilde, Christians may be in the same gutter as everybody else, but we are looking at the stars. Not those illusory will-o'-the-wisps of which secular optimism has spoken, with its spurious dreams of a Utopian heaven on earth brought in by man's political or technological progress. No, the stars which we Christians have our eyes fixed upon are a million times more certain than the best hopes of unbelieving mankind. We are looking forward to glory. And though we have no visible guarantee of its arrival, though all we have to go on is the empty tomb, and the Spirit within us, these things are sufficient to sustain in us an unshakeable conviction of its dependability.

18

A plan that cannot fail

The best laid schemes of mice and men may go oft agley, but not God's scheme. This is a hope that will not disappoint us. This is a plan that will not fail. One day God is going not only to remedy the guilt of sin – he has done that; not only to counteract the power of sin – he is doing that; one day he is going to deliver us from the very *consequences* of sin in us and in our environment. There will be a new heaven and a new earth. It will be glory. And this plan cannot fail. Paul ends this marvellous chapter with a lyrical description of why it cannot fail.

No unforeseen accidents

This great plan, Paul says, cannot fail because it can suffer no unforeseen accidents: 'we know that in all things God works for the good of those who love him, who have been called according to his purpose' (Rom. 8:28). One of the reasons our plans are so prone to failure is that we cannot read the future. And even if by some stroke of clairvoyance we could read the future, we would still have little ability to alter it. But God suffers no such limitations. When he makes a plan, there are no loose ends. No risks, no surprises, no trusting to luck. On the contrary, every detail of the process has been ordered by a sovereign providence to the single goal of achieving his purpose. Nothing can frustrate it. And, says Paul, if you and I have been given a part to play in such a great divine plan, if we have been 'called according to his purpose', we can be absolutely sure that everything that happens to us happens in accordance with that plan, and is overruled by that purpose. Why, then, should those whom God has called to be his own children fear circumstance? Maybe we will encounter suffering. It is inevitable that we will in one way or another. But if so, it will be suffering 'according to his purpose'.

I know miracles happen, but miracles are rare. That is why they are miracles. The day miracles start happening every day will be the day when Jesus has returned. Then, miracles will be natural, not supernatural. But right now the normative experience of a Christian in this present age is 'suffering'. Don't let anybody deceive you about that. Paul does not say, you notice, that all things work together for our comfort or for our pleasure. Those who understand Gethsemane and Calvary know that God moves in mysterious ways, ways that sometimes involve horrendous pain, even for those nearest and dearest to his own divine heart. 'Take up your cross,' says Jesus, 'and follow me.' But when God's plan demands such cross-bearing of us, it is nevertheless for the good of those who love him. It is never futile; it is never malicious. For this great plan which he is at work on suffers no unforeseen accidents. It is masterminded by

irresistible omnipotence and infallible intelligence.
That is the first reason why it cannot fail.

No weak links

The second reason it cannot fail? Because there is
no weak link in its strategy: 'those God foreknew
he also predestined to be conformed to the likeness of his Son, that he might be the firstborn
among many brothers. And those he predestined,
he also called; those he called, he also justified;
those he justified, he also glorified' (Rom. 8:29–30).
They say a chain is only as strong as its weakest
link. Well, here Paul presents us with what some
have called the golden chain. It consists of five
verbs, verbs which in a marvellous way outline
this great Masterplan that we have been thinking
about.

God was determined to adopt a company of
fallen men and women as his own children, Paul
says, to transform them into his own divine image,
and to share glory with them. That is God's plan,
and these are the five stages, says Paul, by which
he did it:

> he foreknew them,
> he predestined them,
> he called them,
> he justified them,
> he glorified them.

First, notice who is the subject of each of those
verbs: God every time. Not one of these five links
is contingent upon human actions that might go

wrong. Every one of them represents a divine action that must go right.

Secondly, notice the tense of each of those verbs. Every one of them is in the past tense, even the last one: 'those he justified, he also glorified'. And we want to say, 'But Paul, you've been stressing so much that we aren't glorified yet. We're still immersed in this sin-sick, suffering world of ours. Surely what you mean to say is, "those he justified, he *will* also glorify".' But no, Paul has not made a mistake in his grammar. The point is that when God purposes to do something, the tense of the verb may be future as far as our experience in time goes, but it is always past as far as God's eternal perspective is concerned. When a sovereign as powerful as he is determines to do something, then the moment the decision is made it is as good as done. Our glorification, then, is not in doubt. It may be a hope, but it is a sure hope, just as strong and reliable a link in the chain of God's purpose as all the others, even though it has not yet happened.

Thirdly, notice the object of these five verbs. For Paul is careful to make plain that it is the same group of people every time. The Greek structure of the verse stresses this very firmly. It is those God foreknew whom he also predestined; those he predestined whom he also called; and so on each time. There are no dropouts on the way. All who are foreknown are predestined; all who are predestined are called; all who are called are justified; all who are justified are glorified, says Paul. Salvation may enter into our experience in chronologically distinct stages, but it is in fact, as far as God is concerned, one single event rendered certain and infallible, not on the day when we eventually make it to glory, not even on the day we believed in Christ and were justified by faith. No, says Paul, this plan was determined infallibly right at the beginning of time. There is no weak link in this chain. From first to last it has been executed and will be executed by God's initiative and power, and there is no possibility of any hiccup in the process.

No power can obstruct God's plan

And the third reason it is a plan that cannot fail? There is no power in the entire universe that can obstruct it.

> What, then, shall we say in response to this? If God is for us, who can be against us? He who did not spare his own Son, but gave him up for us all – how will he not also, along with him, graciously give us all things? Who will bring any charge against those whom God has chosen? It is God who justifies. Who is he that condemns? Christ Jesus, who died – more than that, who was raised to life – is at the right hand of God and is also interceding for us.
>
> (Rom. 8:31–34)

Paul is picturing for us here the final assize, where all of us will stand on trial and give account of ourselves before God's bar of justice. When he asks the rhetorical question, 'Who will bring any charge against those whom God has chosen?', almost certainly, he is anticipating the answer, 'The devil.' For one of the principal roles of the devil in the Bible is as the prosecutor of God's people. The Greek word *diabolos* means 'slanderer'. I have no doubt that the devil, when he inspired men to crucify Christ, thought that he had at last obtained an unanswerable case against mankind. What crime could possibly exceed the murder of God's own Son? It makes Adam's eating of the fruit of the tree of knowledge look trivial by comparison, doesn't it? God must surely condemn them now! He can't put up with their rebellion any longer. The constraints of God's own justice must demand that he destroy them once and for all.

But the devil did not understand the depths of the divine love. He did not understand the subtlety of the divine purpose. For this very God whose Son men killed turned their capital crime into an atoning sacrifice. And the very Christ who was the victim of man's hate rose again, not to join the devil's side as witness for the prosecution and to cry vengeance on his murderers, but to stand with the defendants in the dock as their defending counsel and to plead for their release. 'Here is a Christian,' says Paul. 'Who is going to accuse him, then? God the Father? But he is the Judge and has already declared him righteous on the basis of Jesus' death. God the Son? But he is his advocate, praying unceasingly for the prisoner's pardon. No, the glorious fact is, when a Christian goes on trial, the devil's case for the prosecution collapses.'

It is impossible to imagine that God would have invested so much in a plan to save the Christian only to have it thwarted at the last by some unanswerable satanic accusation. If he was so determined to bring us to glory that he did not withhold the ultimate sacrifice, his own Son, but watched him hang on a cross before the mockery of his own creation for our sake; if God was willing to do that greatest of things, surely there can be no doubting his willingness to do whatever lesser things remain to be done to complete his work of grace in us.

There can be no question about it; there is no one who can obstruct the intended outcome. Our final acquittal is certain. 'Who shall separate us from the love of Christ?' (Rom. 8:35). Paul scans the universe for something – anything in this entire fallen world that can thwart the fulfilment of God's plan; trouble, hardship, persecution, famine, nakedness, danger, sword. The opposition of those hostile ideologies that are antagonistic to the church, that want to put Christians in prison and even kill them – can they do it? Those malicious demonic hosts that want to undermine our holiness, to trap us into sin again – can they do it? The titanic forces of pagan superstition and secular culture that want to corrupt and compromise our testimony – can they do it? Paul surveys it all: every negative and anti-Christian experience and influence that it is possible to imagine. And he draws a magnificent and thrilling blank. He says:

> No, in all these things we are more
> than conquerors through him who

loved us. For I am convinced that neither death nor life, neither angels nor demons, neither the present nor the future, nor any powers, neither height nor depth, nor anything else in all creation, will be able to separate us from the love of God that is in Christ Jesus our Lord.

(Rom. 8:37–39)

God is determined upon it. No unforeseen accident can frustrate it; no weak link in the chain can frustrate it; no power on earth can frustrate it. He is determined to bring us to glory. The plans of mice and men may be suspect, but not the Masterplan. This is one plan that cannot fail.

19

Which way forward?

Some readers of this book may be looking for answers. 'Why am I on this planet? Why are any of us here? Why, amongst the millions of lifeless and unpopulated planets in the universe that have resulted from the Big Bang, did our world emerge? Why did human life emerge?' Paul has the solution. We are here because God has a plan, a plan that cannot fail, and we human beings are at the heart of it. That is why we feel the need to ask 'Why?' If we were just animals the question of ultimate destiny would not matter to us. We would be content simply to survive. We are troubled with unanswered 'why's' buzzing around in our minds because we are more than animals. We are human beings made in the image of God. We were made for a great destiny – to share the glory of God. Can't you hear the voice of your Maker? Millennia ago you were in his mind. Millennia ago this very moment was in his mind, the moment when he would call to you and invite you to find in his plan for your life the answer to those questioning 'why's' in your mind and heart.

Hope

Many people today are looking for hope. It was Woody Allen who made the comment, 'The future isn't what it used to be.' Too right it isn't. Optimism about the destiny of the human race has almost totally collapsed. As we were saying earlier in this book, visions of Utopia that fired an earlier generation lie wrecked under the carnage of dozens of bloody wars and revolutions. Predictions of human progress that motivated scientific research a hundred years ago lie shrouded now in the mushroom cloud of Hiroshima and the pollution of Chernobyl. You will find here and there a few who cling to those old impossible dreams of a man-made paradise on earth, but for the vast majority of people who dare to think realistically rather than gaze through the rose-tinted spectacles of a discredited humanism, such spurious visions are just the secularized equivalent of those false prophets who in Jeremiah's day cried, 'Peace, peace,' when there was no peace.

Kenneth Clarke in his celebrated book *Civilization* writes, 'Confident articles about the future are to my mind the most disreputable of all public utterances.' And as that mystical year 2000 approaches, global insecurity becomes more and more acute. Where are we to turn in such days? To scientists, to politicians? They are the people who have more than anybody else created the insecurity, and they are suffering from the same confusion as we are. I remember talking to an American student some years ago who told me, 'We used to trust the generals, but Vietnam changed all that. We used to trust the politicians, but Watergate changed all that. We used to trust the scientists, but Three-Mile Island changed all that. Now there's nobody we trust.' That's about it. It wouldn't be so bad if you believed there was at least somebody at the top who knew where we were all going. But even that myth lies shattered.

Do you remember that song from *Paint Your Wagon*? 'Where am I going? I don't know. When will I get there? I ain't certain. I only know that I am on my way.' It would be a good signature tune for twentieth-century political leadership. That kind of cavalier enthusiasm for progress, irrespective of any clear sense of direction, is precisely its characteristic. We talk about progress and advance, but we don't know where we're going. Unfortunately our particular wagon is harnessed to an engine of technological expertise which is generating a million pounds of thrust and which has neither brakes nor steering. Our civilization was born not under a wandering star but under a shooting star. And all the signs are that its meteoric career may reach a sudden end. It would be easy to despair, and a lot of people do. But a Christian does not have to. Paul said, 'I consider that our present sufferings are not worth comparing with the glory that will be revealed in us' (Rom. 8:18).

In the year 410 AD Augustine, Bishop of Hippo in North Africa, heard the news that Rome had been sacked. It was the end of civilization as he knew it. His was a world in many respects uncannily like ours, with family breakdowns and escapist entertainments and obsessive sex and violence. But it was an ordered world, a secure world, a civilization that had stood for hundreds of years. Augustine compared the fall of Rome to the destruction of Sodom. And in his sermon he told his congregation that they must not lose heart. There will be an end to every earthly kingdom, he told them. This world is passing away. This world is short of breath. Do not fear. Your youth will be renewed like the eagle's, he said. He knew, you see. He knew that one day God would deliver us from the consequences of sin and give us a new heaven and a new earth to enjoy. He spent the remaining seventeen years of his life completing his greatest book, *The City of God*, a city which, unlike Rome, could never pass away.

I have a suspicion that for those of us who survive to the twenty-first century the most distinctive thing about being a Christian may not in fact be our morality, it will be our hope.

Adventure

Are you looking for adventure? Something to live for? Something that will last for ever? Cynicism is in the air. The yuppie generation has overtaken us. There are no causes left to fire the imagination today. But that doesn't mean that we don't secretly wish for adventures.

Don Marquis wrote about that longing in *The Lesson of the Moth*. Archie, a disillusioned cockroach, describes how unsuccessfully he tried to convince a moth of the foolishness of the latter's determination to break in on an electric lightbulb and 'fry himself' on the wires. The moth replied to Archie:

> It is better to be a part of beauty for one instant and then cease to exist, than to exist forever and never be a part of beauty.

Archie concludes the story:

> Before I could argue him out of his philosophy he went and immolated himself on a patent cigar lighter. I do not agree with him. Myself, I would rather have half the happiness and twice the longevity, but at the same time I wish, I wish there was something I wanted as badly as he wanted to fry himself.

Do you see what Marquis is getting at there? You don't know that you have something worth living for unless you've got something worth dying for. But all the causes worth dying for have fallen. Now that Marxism has collapsed, what else is left? No one is going to die for the New Age movement, I assure you. Just suppose it were even possible to have all the happiness and all the longevity that you can imagine. Would any effort be too much, any sacrifice too great, in order to share the glory of God? That glory is a holy flame that does not destroy but transforms, turning death into life, mortality into eternity.

We Christians have done something in our generation which the early Christians would have found hard to believe. We have made Christianity dull and unexciting. But Christianity isn't dull! It is an invitation to the greatest adventure the world can offer. To quote C. S. Lewis, 'This God is going to take the feeblest and the filthiest of us and turn us into dazzling, radiant, immortal creatures pulsating with all the energy and joy and wisdom and love that we could possibly imagine. He's going to turn us into bright stainless mirrors that reflect back his character perfectly.' That is what we are in for – nothing less. God will settle for nothing less. That is something worth living for!

Then let us go and serve the King!

Dilemmas of Life
Deciding what's right and what's wrong

DAVID COOK

'I just don't know what I ought to do.'

'She ended up choosing the lesser of two evils.'

'At first he stuck to his principles. Now he's beginning to feel it wouldn't be a very loving thing to do.'

Decisions. Questions of right and wrong. They face us every day. Have you ever thought *how* you arrive at your answers? What makes you think something's wrong, when your friend thinks it's right?

David Cook helps us to see how some influential thinkers have tackled these issues. And then he suggests an alternative framework for moral decision-making.

David Cook is Director of the Whitefield Institute (a Christian research centre), a Fellow of Green College, Oxford, and a frequent and witty broadcaster.

112 pages   *'B' format*

Inter-Varsity Press

The Unfolding Mystery
Discovering Christ in the Old Testament
EDMUND P. CLOWNEY

Everybody knows that the Old Testament is full of stories. But many readers of the Old Testament have difficulty in grasping what its story-line is and how, in the long run, the first part of the Bible relates to the New Testament.

Starting with Adam and Eve and continuing to the last of the prophets, Dr Edmund Clowney shows how the Old Testament fits together as an extended build-up for the coming of Christ, the promised redeemer. Here is a book which helps the reader find Christ revealed in the Old Testament without resorting to fanciful interpretations. It both satisfies the mind and warms the heart.

224 pages   *'B' format*

Inter-Varsity Press

Francis A. Schaeffer Trilogy

The God Who Is There
Escape from Reason
He Is There and He Is Not Silent

FRANCIS SCHAEFFER

What is the relevance of historic Christian faith in the late twentieth century? It was in response to modern questions and dilemmas that the three essential books contained in this trilogy were written. Francis Schaeffer's basic thesis, in his own words, is 'that Christianity has balance: that biblical exegesis gives intellectual depths, and also, in the area of practical living and beauty, Christianity has a relation to the whole person. . . . Every area of life is touched by truth and a song.' While revising these books shortly before his death from cancer, Francis Schaeffer wrote: 'They were written to be read and useful to both Christians and non-Christians. Time has proved this to be the case far beyond my hopes.'

Francis Schaeffer was a leading apologist whose books, films and lectures have had a world-wide influence. His books have been translated into more than twenty-five languages with more than three million copies in print.

416 pages   *'B' format*

Inter-Varsity Press